CAMPERVANS, COOKING, AND CORPSES

Delicious Camper-Friendly Meals and Humorous Murder Mysteries—The Perfect Guide for Life on 4 Wheels

HATTIE B. ROWE

TABLE OF CONTENTS

INTRODUCTION

MY JOURNEY INTO THE WORLD OF CAMPERVAN COOKING AND CULINARY MYSTERIES

Picture this: a blustery autumn evening on the Cornish coast, rain pelting the roof of my trusty campervan, Agatha. (Yes, I named her after the queen of mystery herself, Agatha Christie.) There I was, a novice van-lifer with a rumbling tummy and a tin of beans, staring forlornly at my tiny camping stove. Fast forward five years, and I'm whipping up gourmet meals in the same cramped space, all while weaving tales of culinary intrigue. How did I get here? Pull up a camping chair, and let me spill the beans – hopefully not literally this time.

It all began with a midlife crisis of sorts. Bored with my 9-to-5 job in London and nursing an obsession with crime novels, I decided to combine my love for food, mystery, and the great outdoors. I bought Agatha – a beat-up 1985 VW campervan – and set off on a gastronomic tour of the UK. My plan? I want to visit every location featured in my favourite detective novels and recreate the meals mentioned on their pages.

I won't lie to you – the early days were rough. I burned more sausages than I care to admit, and my first attempt at Miss Marple's famous quiche nearly took out a campsite in Devon. But with each mishap came a lesson, and slowly but surely, I began to master the art of cooking in a space smaller than most people's loos.

I learned to balance pots on a single burner, to chop vegetables on a board perched on my lap, and to create three-course meals using nothing but a camping kettle and a dream. I discovered the joy of foraging for ingredients in hedgerows and the thrill of bartering with local farmers for fresh eggs and veg. And all the while, I was piecing together the puzzle of perfect campervan cuisine.

But it wasn't just about the food. As I travelled from the misty moors of Yorkshire to the sun-dappled lanes of Sussex, I found myself collecting stories as readily as recipes. The mysterious disappearance of Mrs. Higgins' prize-winning Victoria Sponge at the village fête in St. Mary Mead. The curious incident of the vanishing venison at a Highland hunting lodge. The case of the poisoned Ploughman's in a Cotswold pub. Each of these 'culinary crimes' added flavour to my journey and spice to my cooking.

And so, dear reader, this cookbook was born – a labour of love simmered over five years of adventures, mishaps, and delicious discoveries. It's the book I wish I'd had when I first set out in Agatha, full of the tips and tricks I've learned the hard way so that you don't have to.

HOW THIS BOOK WILL TRANSFORM YOUR MEALS AND ADVENTURES

Now, you might be wondering, "Why on earth do I need a cookbook that combines campervans, cooking, and corpses?" Fair question. Let me explain why this peculiar blend is the secret ingredient your adventures have been missing.

First and foremost, this isn't just a cookbook – it's a survival guide for the culinarily challenged camper. Whether you're a seasoned van-lifer or a weekend warrior, these pages hold the key to transforming your meals from bland to grand, all within the confines of your mobile kitchen.

Gone are the days of subsisting on pot noodles and soggy sandwiches. With this book in hand, you'll be crafting restaurant-worthy dishes that'll make your campsite neighbours green with envy. Imagine tucking into a steaming bowl of "Rigor Mortis Risotto" as the sun sets over the Scottish Highlands, or starting your day with a plate of "Alibi Avocado Toast" before hitting the road to your next destination.

But it's not just about the food. This book is your ticket to a whole new way of experiencing the great outdoors. Each recipe comes with a side of mystery, a dash of intrigue, and a hefty helping of adventure. As you cook your way through these pages, you'll also be unravelling culinary conundrums and solving gastronomic puzzles. Who says dinner can't be delicious and thrilling?

HERE'S WHAT YOU CAN EXPECT TO FIND WITHIN THESE PAGES:

1. Campervan Cooking 101: We'll start with the basics, covering everything from setting up your mobile kitchen to stocking your van with essential ingredients. You'll learn how to make the most of limited space and resources, turning constraints into creativity.

2. Recipe Chapters: From "Mysterious Morning Meals" to "Desserts to Die For", each chapter is packed with easy-to-follow recipes that are big on flavour but low on fuss. And don't worry – despite the nefarious names, all of these dishes are 100% murder-free.

3. Tips and Tricks: Peppered throughout the book, you'll find "Crime Scene Investigation" boxes filled with handy cooking tips, "Forensic Analysis" sections explaining the science behind cooking techniques, and "Cold Case Files" featuring variations on recipes.

4. Culinary Capers: Each chapter opens with a short mystery story inspired by real-life adventures and mishaps from my travels. These tales not only entertain but also set the scene for the recipes that follow.

5. Practical Advice: From meal planning to food safety on the road, this book covers all aspects of campervan cuisine. You'll find checklists, conversion charts, and even a guide to foraging (without poisoning yourself or your dinner guests).

By the time you've cooked your way through this book, you'll be a master of mobile meal-making. You'll know how to whip up a feast in the most remote locations, how to impress your fellow campers with your culinary skills, and how to turn every meal into an exciting event.

But more than that, you'll have gained a new perspective on travel and food. You'll see every journey as a potential mystery to be solved, every meal as a story waiting to be told. You'll learn to embrace the unexpected, to find humour in kitchen disasters, and to create unforgettable memories around the camping stove.

THE BASICS OF CAMPERVAN LIFE

CHOOSING THE RIGHT CAMPERVAN FOR YOUR CULINARY ADVENTURES

When I first decided to embark on my campervan culinary journey, I thought any old van with four wheels and a cooker would do. Oh, how wrong I was! Choosing the right campervan is like selecting the perfect ingredients for a complex recipe get it wrong, and the whole dish falls flat. So, let me share what I've learned about picking the ideal mobile kitchen on wheels.

SIZE MATTERS

First things first, size is crucial. Now, you might be tempted to go for the biggest van you can afford, dreaming of spacious worktops and a fridge the size of Wales. But remember, bigger isn't always better. A larger van might give you more cooking space, but it'll also be harder to manoeuvre down those charming (read: terrifyingly narrow) country lanes where the best farm shops hide.

My dear Agatha is a compact VW T25. She's small enough to navigate tight spots but roomy enough for me to whip up a three-course meal without developing a severe case of claustrophobia. For solo travellers or couples, I'd recommend something similar. If you're cooking for a family, though, you might want to consider something a bit roomier, like a long-wheelbase van conversion or a small motorhome.

LAYOUT IS KEY

The layout of your van can make or break your culinary adventures. When you're viewing potential campervans, imagine yourself cooking in them. Is there enough counter space to chop vegetables? Is the cooker at a comfortable height? Can you open the fridge door without having to step outside?

In Agatha, I have a small L-shaped kitchen at the back. It's compact, but every inch is usable space. The cooker is right next to the sink, which makes washing up a breeze (well, as much of a breeze as washing up ever is). And crucially, I can reach the fridge without getting out of my seat essential for those midnight snack raids!

COOKING FACILITIES

Speaking of cookers, pay close attention to the cooking facilities in any van you're considering. Most campervans come with a two-burner hob, which is perfectly adequate for most meals. If you're a baking enthusiast, though, you might want to look for a van with a small oven.

Agatha came with a basic two-burner hob and a grill. I later added a portable electric oven, which has been a game-changer for my "Death by Chocolate Lava Cakes". Remember, you can always upgrade your cooking facilities later, but it's much harder to change the basic layout of your van.

POWER SOURCE

Consider how you'll power your culinary creations. Most campervans run on a combination of gas (for cooking and heating) and 12V electrics (for lighting and running the fridge). Some newer models have induction hobs, which are great for cooking but require a hefty battery setup or hook-up to mains electricity.

I've found that a dual-fuel setup works best for me. I use gas for cooking when I'm off-grid, and switch to electric when I'm hooked up at a campsite. This flexibility means I'm never caught short, whether I'm whipping up a quick "Stakeout Stir-fry" in a remote lay-by or spending a week perfecting my "Shallow Grave Soufflé" at a fully-serviced pitch.

STORAGE SOLUTIONS

Finally, don't underestimate the importance of storage. You'll need space for food, cookware, and utensils. Look for vans with plenty of cupboards, drawers, and clever storage solutions. I've added extra shelves and hanging storage to Agatha over the years, turning every nook and cranny into usable space.

Remember, your perfect culinary campervan is out there. Take your time, do your research, and don't be afraid to ask sellers if you can try cooking a simple meal in a van before you buy. After all, you wouldn't buy a house without checking out the kitchen, would you?

ESSENTIAL EQUIPMENT FOR YOUR MOBILE KITCHEN

Now that you've got your perfect culinary campervan, it's time to kit it out. When I first started, I made the rookie mistake of trying to cram my entire kitchen into Agatha. Trust me, you don't need three different sizes of saucepan and that fancy egg poacher you've used exactly once. What you do need is a carefully curated selection of versatile equipment that can handle anything from a quick breakfast to a full-blown dinner party (yes, I've hosted those in my van more on that later!).

COOKING EQUIPMENT
Let's start with the basics:

1. A good quality, non-stick frying pan: This is your best friend in a campervan kitchen. I use mine for everything from frying eggs for my "Alibi Avocado Toast" to searing steaks for my "Crime Scene Steak Diane". Look for one with a removable handle to save space.

2. A medium-sized saucepan with a lid: Perfect for boiling pasta, making sauces, and even baking bread (yes, really!). I once made an entire "Corpus Delicti Cassoulet" in mine.

3. A small saucepan: Ideal for heating soups, making porridge, or creating delicious sauces.

4. A kettle: Essential for your morning brew and a multitude of cooking tasks. I prefer a stovetop kettle as it doesn't require electricity, but an electric one is fine if you're usually on hook-up.

5. A chopping board: Get a flexible, lightweight one that can double as a serving platter.

6. Sharp knives: A chef's knife and a paring knife will cover most of your needs. Don't forget a knife guard for safe storage.

7. Measuring cups and spoons: Crucial to follow recipes accurately in a small space where eyeballing ingredients can lead to disaster.

8. Colander: Look for a collapsible one to save space.

9. Mixing bowls: Again, collapsible is best. I have a set of three that nest inside each other.

10. Wooden spoons, spatula, and tongs: These are your basic utensils. I hang mine on hooks to save drawer space.

FOOD PREPARATION AND STORAGE

1. Airtight containers: Essential for storing leftovers and keeping ingredients fresh. I use a set of nesting containers to save space.

2. Reusable silicone food bags: Great for marinating meats or storing prepped vegetables.

3. A good quality cool box or portable fridge: If your van doesn't have a built-in fridge, this is crucial. I started with a cool box and upgraded to a 12V portable fridge after a year.

4. Herb and spice kit: Pre-fill small containers with your most-used herbs and spices. It'll save you from carrying full-size jars and transform even the simplest meals.

SERVING AND EATING

1. Plates, bowls, and mugs: I prefer enamelware as it's durable and lightweight. Plus, it gives that authentic camping feel!

2. Cutlery: A basic set for however many people usually travel in your van, plus a couple extra for guests.

3. A corkscrew/bottle opener: Because sometimes, solving culinary mysteries is thirsty work.

4. Reusable water bottles: Stay hydrated while reducing plastic waste.

CLEANING UP

1. Washing up bowl: Get one that fits your sink. It saves water and can double as a food prep area in a pinch.

2. Tea towels and dishcloths: More than you think you'll need. Trust me on this one.

3. Biodegradable washing up liquid: Kind to the environment and multi-purpose. I use mine for dishes, laundry, and even as body wash in emergencies!

4. Bin bags and recycling bags: Keep your van clean and tidy.

Remember, this list is a starting point. As you embark on your campervan culinary adventures, you'll figure out what works best for you. Maybe you'll discover you can't live without your spiralizer, or that a mini food processor is the key to the perfect "Poisoned Pesto". The joy of campervan cooking is adapting and innovating embrace it!

SAFETY FIRST: FIRE, GAS, AND FOOD SAFETY IN A CAMPERVAN

Now, I know safety might not be the most thrilling topic when you're dreaming of romantic dinners under the stars or perfecting your "Deadly Nightshade Berry Crumble". But trust me, nothing ruins a campervan culinary adventure faster than a trip to A&E or a bout of food poisoning. So, let's talk about keeping safe while you're cooking up a storm in your home on wheels.

FIRE SAFETY

First things first, fire safety. Your campervan is a cosy space, which means the fire can spread quickly if you're not careful. Here are some essential tips:

1. Install a smoke detector and carbon monoxide alarm: Check the batteries regularly. I change mine every time I change the clocks for daylight savings it's an easy way to remember.

2. Keep a fire extinguisher and fire blanket easily accessible: Make sure you know how to use them. I keep mine right by the door, so I can grab them quickly if needed.

3. Never leave cooking unattended: I know it's tempting to start cooking and then pop outside to enjoy the view but resist the urge. Your "Shallow Grave Shepherd's Pie" isn't worth burning down your van for.

4. Keep flammable items away from the cooker: This includes tea towels, oven gloves, and that stack of true crime novels you're using for inspiration.

5. Allow hot pans and cooking equipment to cool before storing: I learnt this the hard way when I melted a plastic container by putting a hot pan on it. The smell lingered for weeks!

GAS SAFETY

Most campervans use gas for cooking, and while it's generally very safe, it's important to take precautions:

1. Regularly check your gas system: Get it serviced by a professional at least once a year. I do mine every spring, just before the start of peak camping season.

2. Use a gas detector: These nifty devices will alert you to any gas leaks. I have one permanently installed near the floor of my van, as gas is heavier than air and sinks.

3. Always turn off the gas at the cylinder when not in use: This includes when you're driving. It's a simple habit that could save your life.

4. Ensure proper ventilation when cooking: Open a window or vent, especially when using the gas hob. Not only does this reduce condensation, but it also prevents the build-up of potentially harmful gases.

5. Know the signs of carbon monoxide poisoning: Headaches, dizziness, nausea, and confusion can all be symptoms. If you suspect carbon monoxide, get out of the van immediately and seek fresh air.

FOOD SAFETY

Last but certainly not least, let's talk about food safety. The last thing you want is to solve the mystery of "Who Poisoned the Picnic?" only to realise it was your dodgy food handling!

1. Keep your cool: Invest in a good quality cool box or portable fridge. Check the temperature regularly to ensure it's keeping food at 5°C or below.

2. Separate raw and cooked foods: Use different chopping boards and utensils for raw meat and ready-to-eat foods. In a small space, cross-contamination can happen easily if you're not vigilant.

3. Cook food thoroughly: Invest in a food thermometer to ensure meats are cooked to safe temperatures. Your "Corpus Delicti Chicken" should reach at least 75°C at its thickest part.

4. Practice good hand hygiene: Always wash your hands before preparing food, after handling raw meat, and after using the loo. I keep a bottle of alcohol-based hand sanitizer in my van for times when water is scarce.

5. Be water-wise: If you're not sure about the safety of the local water supply, use bottled water for drinking and cooking. I always keep a few litres of bottled water in Agatha, just in case.

6. Mind your leftovers: In a small fridge, it's tempting to keep leftovers for days. Don't. Use them within 2 days and always reheat until piping hot.

7. Check your dates: In a campervan, you might not always have easy access to shops. Check use-by dates when you buy food and plan your meals accordingly.

Remember, a little caution goes a long way in preventing culinary calamities. By following these safety tips, you can ensure that the only mystery in your campervan is "What's for dinner?" and not "Why do I feel so ill?".

CAMPERVAN COOKING TECHNIQUES

When I first started cooking in Agatha, my trusty campervan, I felt like I was trying to recreate a Michelin-starred restaurant in a shoebox. But over time, I've learned that with a bit of creativity and the right techniques, you can create culinary masterpieces even in the cosiest of spaces. Let me share some of the tricks I've picked up along the way.

ONE-BURNER WONDERS: MASTERING LIMITED COOKING SPACE

Ah, the humble campervan hob. Usually sporting just one or two burners, it's a far cry from the multi-ring affairs we're used to in our home kitchens. But fear not, my culinary comrades! With a bit of clever thinking, you can create mouth-watering meals on even the most minimalist of cooking setups.

THE ART OF SEQUENCING

The key to one-burner cooking is all in the sequencing. Think of your meal as a carefully choreographed dance, with each element taking its turn in the spotlight. Here's how I approach it:

1. Start with the longest-cooking item: This is usually your protein or any grains. For instance, when making my "Rigor Mortis Risotto", I start by cooking the rice.

2. Use residual heat: Once your main item is cooked, set it aside wrapped in a tea towel or a thermal container to keep warm. The residual heat will continue to cook it gently.

3. Quick-cook items last: Vegetables, especially greens, cook quickly and are best done just before serving.

ONE-POT MEALS ARE YOUR FRIEND

Embrace one-pot meals. They're not just easy to cook; they're also a doddle to clean up afterwards. Some of my favourites include:

Corpus Delicti Chilli Con Carne: A hearty, spicy one-pot wonder that's perfect for chilly evenings.
Shallow Grave Shakshuka: Eggs poached in a rich tomato sauce a breakfast of champions or a light dinner.
Last Gasp Lentil Curry: A comforting, protein-packed meal that's both delicious and budget-friendly.

LAYERING FLAVOURS

When you're limited to one pot, layering flavours becomes crucial. Start by sautéing aromatic vegetables like onions and garlic. Then add your spices and let them toast for a minute before adding other ingredients. This builds a deep, complex flavour base that will elevate your one-pot meal from simple to sublime.

CLEVER USES FOR YOUR CAMPING KETTLE

Don't underestimate the humble kettle! This versatile piece of equipment is more than just a vessel for your morning cuppa. Here are some clever ways I've found to use a kettle in campervan cooking:

REHYDRATING AND COOKING

1. Instant noodles and couscous Perfect for a quick "Stakeout Supper".
2. Dried mushrooms: Rehydrate them for an umami boost in your "Forest Floor Risotto".
3. Dehydrated camping meals: Great for when you're short on time or energy.

BLANCHING VEGETABLES

Pour boiling water over vegetables like green beans or broccoli, leave for a minute, then drain and refresh in cold water. It's a great way to par-cook veg before adding to stir-fries or salads.

MAKING SIMPLE SAUCES

Use your kettle to make instant gravy, cheese sauce (just add boiling water to a mix of grated cheese and cornflour), or even a simple custard for your "Death by Chocolate Trifle".

CLEANING TRICKS

Boiling water is great for sterilising chopping boards and cleaning stubborn pans. Just be careful when pouring!

FOIL PACKET COOKING FOR EASY CLEANUP

Foil packet cooking is a game-changer for campervan chefs. Not only does it make for easy cleanup, but it also allows you to cook several different things at once on a single burner. Here's how to master this technique:

THE BASIC TECHNIQUE

1. Tear off a sheet of heavy-duty foil, about 30cm long.
2. Place your ingredients in the centre of the foil.
3. Bring the long sides of the foil up and fold them together, creating a sealed seam.
4. Fold up the shorter ends to create a sealed packet.
5. Cook on your hob, turning occasionally, or place in your portable oven if you have one.

SOME FOIL PACKET FAVOURITES

Buried Treasure Salmon: Salmon fillet with lemon slices, dill, and butter.
Campsite Ratatouille: A medley of summer vegetables with herbs and olive oil.
Starry Night S'mores: A dessert packet with crushed biscuits, chocolate, and marshmallows.

TIPS FOR FOIL PACKET SUCCESS

Double up on foil for ingredients that might puncture the packet, like a chicken with bones.
Add a splash of liquid (wine, stock, or water) to create steam and prevent burning.
Remember, food steams in the packets, so it won't brown. If you want crispy edges, open the packets for the last few minutes of cooking.

NO-COOK MEALS FOR HOT DAYS OR LAZY EVENINGS

Sometimes, after a long day of adventuring (or solving culinary crimes), the last thing you want to do is fire up the stove. That's where no-cook meals come in handy. Here are some of my go-to options:

SALADS WITH SUBSTANCE

Stakeout Salad Niçoise: Tinned tuna, boiled eggs (you can buy these pre-cooked), green beans, olives, and tomatoes on a bed of lettuce.

Witness Protection Chickpea Salad: Tinned chickpeas mixed with diced cucumber, tomatoes, feta cheese, and a simple lemon dressing.

SANDWICH SENSATIONS

Cold Case Caprese Sandwich: Sliced mozzarella, tomatoes, and fresh basil leaves drizzled with balsamic glaze on crusty bread.

Undercover Agent's Ploughman's: A classic British picnic lunch with cheese, ham, pickles, and crusty bread.

DIPS AND SNACKS

Alibi Avocado Dip: Mash ripe avocados with lime juice, salt, and pepper for an instant guacamole.

Interrogation Room Hummus Platter: Shop-bought hummus served with carrot sticks, cucumber slices, and pitta bread.

OVERNIGHT SENSATIONS

Prepare these the night before for a delicious no-cook breakfast or lunch:

Corpse-Cold Overnight Oats: Mix oats with milk (dairy or plant-based), yoghurt, and your choice of fruit and nuts. Leave in the fridge overnight for a creamy, delicious breakfast.

Shallow Grave Gazpacho: Blend ripe tomatoes with cucumber, peppers, garlic, and olive oil. Chill overnight for a refreshing cold soup.

Remember, no-cook doesn't mean any taste! With a bit of creativity and some clever ingredient choices, you can create delicious meals without ever turning on the stove.

Whether you're mastering one-burner meals, getting creative with your kettle, perfecting foil packet dinners, or embracing no-cook options, these techniques will help you make the most of your campervan kitchen.

CREATING FLEXIBLE MEAL PLANS FOR YOUR JOURNEY

When I first hit the road in Agatha, my meal planning was about as organized as a crime scene before the forensics team arrived. I'd either over-pack, leaving me with a fridge full of wilted veg at the end of the trip, or under-pack and find myself surviving on crisps and chocolate bars. But over time, I've cracked the code of flexible meal planning for campervan life.

THE 3-3-3 METHOD

I swear by what I call the 3-3-3 method:

1. 3 Meals You Can Make from Shelf-Stable Ingredients: Think pasta with tinned tomatoes and herbs, or a hearty bean chilli.
2. 3 Meals That Use Fresh Ingredients: These are for the first few days of your trip. Think stir-fries, fresh salads, or grilled fish.
3. 3 Meals That Can Be Made from Either: These are your flexible meals that can adapt based on what's available. A frittata, for instance, can use fresh veg if you have it, or tinned if you don't.

This method ensures you're prepared for anything, whether you find a brilliant farm shop or end up in the middle of nowhere.

PLAN YOUR MEALS, NOT YOUR DAYS

Instead of assigning meals to specific days, I create a list of meals I can make with the ingredients I have. This allows for flexibility based on your mood, the weather, or what fresh ingredients you manage to pick up along the way.

THE "INGREDIENT TETRIS" GAME

Think of your ingredients as Tetris blocks. How can they fit together in different ways to create varied meals? For example:

Tinned tomatoes can be the base for pasta sauce, soup, or shakshuka.
A pack of mince can become bolognese, chilli, or burgers.
Eggs are the ultimate flexible ingredient for frittatas, carbonara, or a simple scramble.

SHOPPING TIPS FOR REMOTE LOCATIONS

Shopping on the road is an adventure in itself. Here are some tips I've picked up:

KNOW YOUR STAPLES

Always keep a stock of versatile, long-life ingredients. My essentials include:

Pasta, rice, and oats
Tinned tomatoes, beans, and tuna
Olive oil, salt, and a basic spice kit
Onions and garlic (they last ages and add flavour to everything)
UHT milk or non-dairy alternative

EMBRACE LOCAL SHOPS

Village shops and small supermarkets can be treasure troves. They often stock local produce that's fresher and cheaper than what you'd find in big supermarkets.

FARMERS' MARKETS AND FARM SHOPS

These are brilliant for fresh, seasonal produce. I plan my route to hit local markets where possible. Just be prepared for some unusual veg that might inspire new recipes!

THE FREEZER IS YOUR FRIEND

If your campervan has a freezer, use it! Frozen veg, meat, and fish can be lifesavers when fresh isn't available.

LEARN TO LOVE TINNED FISH

Tinned sardines, mackerel, and salmon are nutritious, long-lasting, and don't need refrigeration. They're perfect for quick protein hits on the road.

FORAGING SAFELY: A BEGINNER'S GUIDE

Foraging can add a thrilling element to your campervan cooking, but it's crucial to do it safely and responsibly.

START WITH EASY-TO-IDENTIFY PLANTS

Begin with plants that are distinctive and have no poisonous lookalikes. Some safe bets for beginners include:

Blackberries (late summer to early autumn)
Wild garlic (spring)
Nettles (spring and early summer wear gloves!)
Dandelions (all year round)

INVEST IN A GOOD FIELD GUIDE

A reliable foraging guidebook is worth its weight in gold. I never go foraging without my trusty copy of "Food for Free" by Richard Mabey.

FOLLOW THE FORAGER'S CODE

1. Only take what you need
2. Don't uproot plants
3. Avoid foraging in protected areas or private property without permission
4. Don't forage from polluted areas (e.g., roadsides)

WHEN IN DOUBT, DON'T PICK

If you're not 100% sure what a plant is, leave it be. No meal is worth the risk of poisoning.
Wash Everything Thoroughly
Even if you're planning to cook your foraged finds, always wash them thoroughly first.

THE 'CORPSE' IN COOKING: FOOD SAFETY ON THE ROAD

Now, let's talk about keeping your ingredients from becoming, well, corpses. Food safety is crucial in any kitchen, but it's especially important when you're working with limited space and potentially unreliable refrigeration.

UNDERSTANDING FOOD SPOILAGE AND CONTAMINATION

Food spoilage is when food deteriorates and is no longer fit to eat. Contamination, on the other hand, is when harmful bacteria, viruses, or other microorganisms get into your food. Both can make you seriously ill, turning your campervan culinary adventure into a real-life murder mystery.

THE USUAL SUSPECTS

The main culprits in food spoilage and contamination are:

1. Bacteria: These multiply rapidly in the 'danger zone' between 5°C and 63°C.

2. Enzymes: Natural enzymes in food can cause ripening and eventual spoilage.

3. Oxidation: This causes fats to go rancid and fruits to brown.

4. Physical damage: Bruising or cutting can speed up spoilage.

SIGNS OF SPOILAGE

Always check your food before using it. Look out for:

Mould growth

Unusual smells

Sliminess or unusual texture

Discolouration

Remember, when in doubt, throw it out! It's better to lose an ingredient than to risk food poisoning.

PROPER FOOD STORAGE IN LIMITED SPACE

Storage is key to preventing both spoilage and contamination. Here's how I keep things ship-shape in Agatha:

TEMPERATURE CONTROL

Keep your fridge below 5°C. Use a fridge thermometer to check regularly.

Store raw meat on the bottom shelf to prevent drips from contaminating other foods.

Don't overpack the fridge air needs to circulate to keep everything cool.

SMART PACKING

Use airtight containers or resealable bags to prevent cross-contamination.

Label everything with the date you opened it.

Follow the "first in, first out" rule and use older items before newer ones.

DRY GOODS STORAGE

Store dry goods in airtight containers to keep out moisture and pests.
Keep onions and potatoes in a cool, dark place but not together, as onions can make potatoes sprout faster.

CLEVER CAMPERVAN TRICKS

Use a cool box as extra fridge space on hot days.
Freeze water bottles to use as ice packs as they melt, you have drinking water.
In cooler weather, use the 'boot fridge' the coolest part of your van that can store veg that doesn't need refrigeration.

HANDLING RAW INGREDIENTS SAFELY

Proper handling of raw ingredients is crucial to prevent the spread of harmful bacteria.

THE GOLDEN RULES

1. Wash your hands: Before and after handling food, especially raw meat.
2. Use separate chopping boards: One for raw meat, and one for ready-to-eat foods.
3. Clean as you go: Wipe down surfaces regularly with hot, soapy water.

COOKING TEMPERATURES

Invest in a food thermometer and make sure your food reaches these safe internal temperatures:

Beef, lamb, pork: 63°C
Poultry: 75°C
Fish: 63°C or until flesh is opaque and flakes easily

COOLING AND REHEATING

Cool cooked food quickly (within 1-2 hours) and refrigerate.
When reheating, make sure the food is piping hot all the way through.
Only reheat food once.

Remember, food safety might not be the most exciting part of campervan cooking, but it's certainly one of the most important. After all, the only mystery we want in our meals is "How did something this delicious come from such a tiny kitchen?" not "What on earth made me so ill?".

HAPPY COOKING, AND STAY SAFE OUT THERE, MY CULINARY DETECTIVES!

CHAPTER 1: MYSTERIOUS MORNING MEALS

ALIBI AVOCADO TOAST

Prep: 5 mins | Cook: 5 mins | Serves: 2

Cooking Function: Air Fryer Toast

Ingredients:

UK: 2 slices of sourdough bread, 1 avocado (mashed), 1 teaspoon lemon juice, pinch of chilli flakes, salt and pepper, 2 poached eggs (optional)

US: 2 slices sourdough bread, 1 avocado, 1 teaspoon lemon juice, pinch of red pepper flakes, salt and pepper, 2 poached eggs (optional)

Instructions:

1. Toast the sourdough slices in the air fryer using the Toast function at 180°C (350°F) for 3-4 minutes until golden.
2. In a bowl, mash the avocado with lemon juice, chilli flakes, salt, and pepper.
3. Spread the avocado mixture generously over the toasted bread.
4. Add a poached egg on top if you're preparing for a long morning—because every alibi needs stamina!

Nutritional Info: Calories: 300 | Fat: 20g | Carbs: 24g | Protein: 8g

CORPSE-COLD OVERNIGHT OATS

Prep: 5 mins (plus overnight) | Cook: None | Serves: 2

Cooking Function: None required

Ingredients:

UK: 100g rolled oats, 250ml almond milk, 1 tablespoon chia seeds, 2 teaspoons honey, fresh berries (for topping)

US: 1 cup rolled oats, 1 cup almond milk, 1 tablespoon chia seeds, 2 teaspoons honey, fresh berries

Instructions:

1. Combine oats, almond milk, chia seeds, and honey in a jar and stir well.
2. Seal the jar and let it chill overnight in the fridge—cold like the morning's first crime scene!
3. In the morning, stir the oats and top with fresh berries.
4. Serve cold and enjoy—just the thing for a case you want to solve before breakfast.

Nutritional Info: Calories: 250 | Fat: 6g | Carbs: 40g | Protein: 7g

SMUGGLER'S BREAKFAST BURRITO

Prep: 10 mins | Cook: 8 mins | Serves: 2

Cooking Function: Air Fryer Grill

Ingredients:

UK: 2 large tortillas, 4 eggs, 50g cheddar cheese (grated), 1 red pepper (diced), 1 tablespoon olive oil, salsa (for serving)

US: 2 large tortillas, 4 eggs, 1.8 oz cheddar, 1 bell pepper, 1 tablespoon olive oil

Instructions:

1. Scramble the eggs and stir in the diced red pepper.
2. Divide the eggs and cheese between the tortillas, roll them up tightly, and secure them with toothpicks.
3. Use the Grill function on your air fryer at 200°C (400°F) to grill the burritos for 5 minutes.
4. Serve with salsa and enjoy—just the thing for snuggling your way through the day!

Nutritional Info: Calories: 400 | Fat: 22g | Carbs: 30g | Protein: 18g

DETECTIVE'S DELIGHT PANCAKES

Prep: 5 mins | Cook: 15 mins | Serves: 4

Cooking Function: Air Fryer Bake

Ingredients:

UK: 150g self-raising flour, 2 tablespoons sugar, 1 egg, 200ml milk, 1 teaspoon vanilla extract, butter (for greasing)

US: 1¼ cups flour, 2 tablespoons sugar, 1 egg, ¾ cup milk, 1 teaspoon vanilla

Instructions:

1. Whisk together the flour, sugar, egg, milk, and vanilla until smooth.
2. Grease a small baking dish with butter and pour in some batter.
3. Set the air fryer to Bake function at 180°C (350°F) and cook each pancake for 5-7 minutes until fluffy.
4. Serve stacked high—like evidence piling up in the detective's case!

Nutritional Info: Calories: 150 | Fat: 4g | Carbs: 25g | Protein: 4g

STAKEOUT SHAKSHUKA

Prep: 10 mins | Cook: 20 mins | Serves: 2

Cooking Function: Air Fryer Bake

Ingredients:

UK: 1 onion (diced), 2 garlic cloves (minced), 1 red pepper (sliced), 400g tinned tomatoes, 4 eggs, 1 tablespoon olive oil, salt and pepper

US: 1 onion, 2 garlic cloves, 1 bell pepper, 14 oz canned tomatoes, 4 eggs, 1 tablespoon olive oil

Instructions:

1. Use the Bake function on the air fryer at 180°C (350°F) to sauté the onion, garlic, and peppers for 10 minutes.
2. Add the tinned tomatoes and cook for 5 more minutes.
3. Create small wells in the sauce and crack an egg into each one.
4. Bake for another 5 minutes until the eggs are just set. This dish keeps you sharp during any morning stakeout!

Nutritional Info: Calories: 200 | Fat: 10g | Carbs: 15g | Protein: 12g

WITNESS PROTECTION WAFFLES

Prep: 10 mins | Cook: 10 mins | Serves: 4

Cooking Function: Air Fryer Waffle Iron

Ingredients:

UK: 200g plain flour, 2 teaspoons baking powder, 1 tablespoon sugar, 2 eggs, 250ml milk, butter (for greasing)

US: 1½ cups flour, 2 teaspoons baking powder, 1 tablespoon sugar, 2 eggs, 1 cup milk

Instructions:

1. Whisk together the flour, baking powder, sugar, eggs, and milk until smooth.
2. Preheat your air fryer waffle iron and grease it with butter.
3. Pour in the batter and cook for 8-10 minutes until crisp.
4. Enjoy these waffles in disguise—they might be your best cover yet!

Nutritional Info: Calories: 280 | Fat: 8g | Carbs: 40g | Protein: 8g

CRIME SCENE FRITTATA

Prep: 10 mins | Cook: 15 mins | Serves: 4

Cooking Function: Air Fryer Bake

Ingredients:

UK: 6 eggs, 100ml milk, 1 onion (diced), 1 courgette (grated), 50g feta (crumbled)

US: 6 eggs, ½ cup milk, 1 onion, 1 zucchini, 1.8 oz feta

Instructions:

1. Whisk the eggs and milk together in a bowl.
2. Stir in the onion, courgette, and feta.
3. Use the Bake function on the air fryer at 180°C (350°F) to cook the mixture in an ovenproof dish for 15 minutes.
4. Slice into wedges—this frittata cracks the case of morning hunger!

Nutritional Info: Calories: 180 | Fat: 12g | Carbs: 5g | Protein: 12g

FINGERPRINT FRUIT SALAD

Prep: 10 mins | Cook: None | Serves: 4

Cooking Function: None

Ingredients:

UK: 1 apple (sliced), 1 orange (peeled and segmented), 150g grapes, 1 banana (sliced), 100g strawberries (quartered), 2 tablespoons honey, 1 teaspoon lemon juice

US: 1 apple, 1 orange, 1 cup grapes, 1 banana, ¾ cup strawberries, 2 tablespoons honey, 1 teaspoon lemon juice

Instructions:

1. Combine all the fruit in a large bowl.
2. Drizzle with honey and lemon juice, then toss gently to coat.
3. Serve immediately—light, sweet, and bursting with evidence of a healthy morning!

Nutritional Info: Calories: 120 | Fat: 0.5g | Carbs: 30g | Protein: 1g

INTERROGATION ROOM BREAKFAST SANDWICH

Prep: 5 mins | Cook: 10 mins | Serves: 2

Cooking Function: Air Fryer Toast

Ingredients:

UK: 2 English muffins (halved), 2 eggs, 2 slices cheddar, 2 rashers of bacon, butter (for spreading)

US: 2 English muffins, 2 eggs, 2 slices cheddar, 2 strips bacon, butter

Instructions:

1. Use the Toast function on the air fryer at 180°C (350°F) to lightly toast the muffin halves.
2. Fry the eggs and bacon using the Air Fryer Fry function at 190°C (375°F) for 8 minutes.
3. Assemble the sandwich: butter the muffins, and add cheese, bacon, and eggs.
4. Serve hot—just in time for your interrogation!

Nutritional Info: Calories: 380 | Fat: 20g | Carbs: 28g | Protein: 18g

UNDERCOVER GRANOLA

Prep: 5 mins | Cook: 15 mins | Serves: 8

Cooking Function: Air Fryer Roast

Ingredients:

UK: 250g oats, 50g almonds (sliced), 50g raisins, 3 tablespoons honey, 2 tablespoons coconut oil

US: 2 ½ cups oats, ½ cup almonds, ½ cup raisins, 3 tablespoons honey, 2 tablespoons coconut oil

Instructions:

1. Mix the oats, almonds, honey, and melted coconut oil in a bowl.
2. Spread the mixture in the air fryer basket and use the Roast function at 160°C (320°F) for 15 minutes, stirring halfway.
3. Stir in the raisins once cooled. Store in an airtight jar—this granola stays undercover till you need it!

Nutritional Info: Calories: 210 | Fat: 8g | Carbs: 30g | Protein: 5g

BODY BAG BREAKFAST PORRIDGE

Prep: 2 mins | Cook: 5 mins | Serves: 2

Cooking Function: Air Fryer Reheat

Ingredients:

UK: 100g rolled oats, 500ml milk, 1 tablespoon honey, 1 teaspoon cinnamon, fresh berries (for topping)

US: 1 cup rolled oats, 2 cups milk, 1 tablespoon honey, 1 teaspoon cinnamon

Instructions:

1. Combine the oats, milk, honey, and cinnamon in a bowl.
2. Use the Reheat function on the air fryer at 150°C (300°F) to cook for 5 minutes, stirring halfway.
3. Top with fresh berries and serve—a hearty breakfast to revive anyone!

Nutritional Info: Calories: 180 | Fat: 4g | Carbs: 30g | Protein: 6g

CORONER'S COFFEE CAKE

Prep: 10 mins | Cook: 20 mins | Serves: 6

Cooking Function: Air Fryer Bake

Ingredients:

UK: 150g plain flour, 100g sugar, 1 teaspoon baking powder, 2 eggs, 100g butter (melted), 1 teaspoon cinnamon, 50g walnuts (chopped)

US: 1 ¼ cups flour, ½ cup sugar, 1 teaspoon baking powder, 2 eggs, ½ cup butter, 1 teaspoon cinnamon, ½ cup walnuts

Instructions:

1. Mix the flour, sugar, baking powder, cinnamon, and walnuts in a bowl.
2. Stir in the eggs and melted butter until smooth.
3. Use the Bake function on the air fryer at 170°C (340°F) and cook for 20 minutes.
4. Enjoy with your morning coffee—it's worth every autopsy!

Nutritional Info: Calories: 300 | Fat: 15g | Carbs: 35g | Protein: 5g

CHALK OUTLINE CHIA PUDDING

Prep: 5 mins (plus overnight) | Cook: None | Serves: 2

Cooking Function: None

Ingredients:

UK: 3 tablespoons chia seeds, 250ml almond milk, 1 teaspoon honey, 1 teaspoon vanilla extract, fresh fruit (for topping)

US: 3 tablespoons chia seeds, 1 cup almond milk, 1 teaspoon honey, 1 teaspoon vanilla

Instructions:

1. Mix the chia seeds, almond milk, honey, and vanilla in a jar.
2. Refrigerate overnight, allowing the mixture to thicken.
3. In the morning, stir well and top with fresh fruit.
4. It's a breakfast so perfect, it leaves an impression!

Nutritional Info: Calories: 180 | Fat: 8g | Carbs: 20g | Protein: 4g

CHAPTER 2: LUNCHTIME INVESTIGATIONS

COLD CASE PASTA SALAD

Prep: 15 mins | Cook: 10 mins | Serves: 4

Cooking Function: Air Fryer Boil

Ingredients:

UK: 250g penne pasta, 100g cherry tomatoes (halved), 50g black olives (sliced), 100g mozzarella balls, 2 tablespoons olive oil, 1 tablespoon balsamic vinegar, salt and pepper

US: 2 ½ cups penne, ½ cup cherry tomatoes, ¼ cup black olives, ½ cup mozzarella balls, 2 tablespoons olive oil, 1 tablespoon balsamic vinegar

Instructions:

1. Boil the pasta using the Boil function on the air fryer at 180°C (355°F) for 10 minutes. Drain and let it cool.
2. Toss the cooled pasta with tomatoes, olives, and mozzarella in a large bowl.
3. Drizzle with olive oil and balsamic vinegar, and season with salt and pepper.
4. Chill until ready to serve—deliciously cool and perfect for cracking cases on the go!

Nutritional Info: Calories: 320 | Fat: 10g | Carbs: 42g | Protein: 12g

STASHED CASH SANDWICH

Prep: 5 mins | Cook: 10 mins | Serves: 2

Cooking Function: Air Fryer Toast

Ingredients:

UK: 4 slices wholemeal bread, 2 tablespoons mustard, 4 slices ham, 4 slices cheddar, 2 gherkins (sliced), butter

US: 4 slices whole wheat bread, 2 tablespoons mustard, 4 slices ham, 4 slices cheddar, 2 pickles, butter

Instructions:

1. Butter the bread slices and spread mustard on the other side.
2. Layer ham, cheese, and gherkin slices between two pieces of bread.
3. Use the Toast function on the air fryer at 180°C (355°F) for 8-10 minutes until golden.
4. Serve hot—a sandwich with layers of flavour, just like a hidden stash!

Nutritional Info: Calories: 380 | Fat: 18g | Carbs: 28g | Protein: 20g

POISON IVY PESTO WRAP

Prep: 10 mins | Cook: 5 mins | Serves: 2

Cooking Function: Air Fryer Grill

Ingredients:

UK: 2 large tortilla wraps, 50g pesto, 100g grilled chicken, 50g rocket, 2 tablespoons pine nuts, 50g grated Parmesan

US: 2 large tortillas, ¼ cup pesto, ½ cup grilled chicken, 2 cups arugula, 2 tablespoons pine nuts, ½ cup Parmesan

Instructions:

1. Spread pesto over each wrap. Layer with grilled chicken, rocket, pine nuts, and Parmesan.
2. Roll the wraps tightly and place them in the air fryer.
3. Use the Grill function at 200°C (400°F) for 5 minutes until lightly crisp.
4. Slice and serve—beware, it's addictively good!

Nutritional Info: Calories: 450 | Fat: 25g | Carbs: 30g | Protein: 22g

EVIDENCE BAG QUINOA BOWL

Prep: 10 mins | Cook: 15 mins | Serves: 2

Cooking Function: Air Fryer Steam

Ingredients:

UK: 150g quinoa, 200ml water, 1 avocado (sliced), 100g cherry tomatoes, 50g feta, 1 tablespoon olive oil, 1 teaspoon lemon juice

US: ¾ cup quinoa, 1 cup water, 1 avocado, ½ cup cherry tomatoes, ¼ cup feta

Instructions:

1. Steam the quinoa using the Steam function at 180°C (355°F) for 15 minutes. Fluff with a fork.
2. Arrange the avocado, tomatoes, and feta on top of the quinoa.
3. Drizzle with olive oil and lemon juice before serving—fresh and perfect evidence of a healthy lunch!

Nutritional Info: Calories: 320 | Fat: 18g | Carbs: 32g | Protein: 9g

LINEUP LENTIL SOUP

Prep: 10 mins | Cook: 20 mins | Serves: 4

Cooking Function: Air Fryer Simmer

Ingredients:

UK: 200g red lentils, 1 onion (diced), 2 carrots (chopped), 2 garlic cloves (minced), 1 litre vegetable stock, 1 teaspoon cumin

US: 1 cup red lentils, 1 onion, 2 carrots, 2 garlic cloves, 4 cups vegetable stock, 1 teaspoon cumin

Instructions:

1. Sauté the onions, garlic, and carrots using the Simmer function at 180°C (355°F) for 5 minutes.
2. Add the lentils, cumin, and stock, then simmer for 15 minutes.
3. Serve hot—a hearty soup to line them all up!

Nutritional Info: Calories: 250 | Fat: 2g | Carbs: 40g | Protein: 12g

MISDEMEANOR MINESTRONE

Prep: 15 mins | Cook: 25 mins | Serves: 6

Cooking Function: Air Fryer Simmer

Ingredients:

UK: 200g pasta shells, 2 courgettes (diced), 1 onion (chopped), 2 garlic cloves, 1 litre vegetable stock, 400g chopped tomatoes, 1 teaspoon oregano

US: 2 cups pasta shells, 2 zucchinis, 1 onion, 2 garlic cloves, 4 cups vegetable stock, 14oz canned tomatoes

Instructions:

1. Sauté the onion and garlic with the Simmer function at 190°C (375°F) for 5 minutes.
2. Add courgettes, tomatoes, and stock, and simmer for 20 minutes.
3. Stir in the pasta shells and cook until tender—a soup to confess your love for!

Nutritional Info: Calories: 280 | Fat: 4g | Carbs: 48g | Protein: 10g

CONSPIRACY THEORY COUSCOUS SALAD

Prep: 10 mins | Cook: 5 mins | Serves: 4

Cooking Function: Air Fryer Steam

Ingredients:

UK: 200g couscous, 250ml boiling water, 1 cucumber (diced), 100g cherry tomatoes, 50g feta, 2 tablespoons olive oil, 1 teaspoon lemon juice

US: 1 cup couscous, 1 cup boiling water, 1 cucumber, ½ cup cherry tomatoes, ¼ cup feta

Instructions:

1. Add couscous to a bowl and pour over boiling water. Cover and steam using the Steam function for 5 minutes.

2. Fluff the couscous and mix it with cucumber, tomatoes, and feta.

3. Drizzle with olive oil and lemon juice—a salad with suspiciously good flavour!

Nutritional Info: Calories: 240 | Fat: 12g | Carbs: 28g | Protein: 8g

RANSOM NOTE RAMEN

Prep: 10 mins | Cook: 15 mins | Serves: 2

Cooking Function: Air Fryer Boil

Ingredients:

UK: 200g ramen noodles, 1 litre vegetable broth, 100g mushrooms (sliced), 2 eggs, 2 spring onions (chopped), 2 tablespoons soy sauce, 1 tablespoon sesame oil

US: 7oz ramen noodles, 4 cups vegetable broth, 1 cup mushrooms, 2 eggs, 2 green onions, 2 tablespoons soy sauce, 1 tablespoon sesame oil

Instructions:

1. Boil the noodles using the Boil function at 180°C (355°F) for 5 minutes. Set aside.

2. In the air fryer, simmer the broth with mushrooms for 10 minutes.

3. Soft-boil the eggs in the air fryer at 180°C (355°F) for 6 minutes, then peel and halve.

4. Divide noodles into bowls, ladle in the broth, and top with eggs, spring onions, soy sauce, and a drizzle of sesame oil. A ransom you'll gladly pay!

Nutritional Info: Calories: 400 | Fat: 14g | Carbs: 50g | Protein: 15g

WITNESS STATEMENT WHITE BEAN DIP

Prep: 10 mins | Cook: 0 mins | Serves: 6

Cooking Function: Air Fryer Pulse (Blender Mode)

Ingredients:

UK: 400g white beans (drained), 2 tablespoons olive oil, 1 garlic clove, 1 tablespoon lemon juice, 1 teaspoon cumin, salt and pepper

US: 14oz white beans, 2 tablespoons olive oil, 1 garlic clove, 1 tablespoon lemon juice, 1 teaspoon cumin

Instructions:

1. Combine all ingredients in the air fryer blender using the Pulse function until smooth.
2. Adjust seasoning to taste and serve with pita or veggie sticks—a smooth-talking dip!

Nutritional Info: Calories: 120 | Fat: 5g | Carbs: 15g | Protein: 6g

UNDERCOVER AGENT EGG SALAD

Prep: 10 mins | Cook: 10 mins | Serves: 4

Cooking Function: Air Fryer Boil

Ingredients:

UK: 6 eggs, 100g mayonnaise, 1 teaspoon mustard, 1 celery stick (chopped), salt and pepper, chives (for garnish)

US: 6 eggs, ½ cup mayonnaise, 1 teaspoon mustard, 1 celery stalk

Instructions:

1. Boil the eggs using the Boil function at 180°C (355°F) for 10 minutes. Peel and chop.
2. Mix the eggs with mayonnaise, mustard, celery, and season to taste.
3. Serve on toast or in a sandwich—disguised as a simple salad but packed with flavour!

Nutritional Info: Calories: 230 | Fat: 18g | Carbs: 2g | Protein: 12g

GETAWAY CAR GAZPACHO

Prep: 10 mins | Cook: 0 mins | Serves: 4

Cooking Function: Air Fryer Blend

Ingredients:

UK: 500g ripe tomatoes, 1 cucumber (peeled), 1 red pepper (deseeded), 2 garlic cloves, 3 tablespoons olive oil, 2 tablespoons vinegar, salt and pepper

US: 1lb tomatoes, 1 cucumber, 1 bell pepper, 2 garlic cloves, ¼ cup olive oil, 2 tablespoons vinegar

Instructions:

1. Add all ingredients to the air fryer and blend using the Blend function until smooth.

2. Chill in the fridge for at least an hour before serving—a cool way to make a fast getaway!

Nutritional Info: Calories: 150 | Fat: 10g | Carbs: 14g | Protein: 3g

BURIED TREASURE BAKED POTATO

Prep: 5 mins | Cook: 45 mins | Serves: 2

Cooking Function: Air Fryer Roast

Ingredients:

UK: 2 large baking potatoes, 2 tablespoons olive oil, salt, 50g sour cream, 50g grated cheddar, 2 spring onions (chopped)

US: 2 large baking potatoes, 2 tablespoons olive oil, ¼ cup sour cream, ¼ cup cheddar

Instructions:

1. Rub the potatoes with olive oil and salt, and roast using the Roast function at 200°C (400°F) for 45 minutes.

2. Split the potatoes open and fill with sour cream, cheddar, and spring onions.

3. Enjoy as you dig through layers of flavour!

Nutritional Info: Calories: 300 | Fat: 12g | Carbs: 42g | Protein: 8g

SMOKE SCREEN STUFFED PEPPERS

Prep: 10 mins | Cook: 20 mins | Serves: 4

Cooking Function: Air Fryer Bake

Ingredients:

UK: 4 bell peppers (halved and deseeded), 200g cooked rice, 100g black beans, 50g sweetcorn, 1 teaspoon smoked paprika, 50g grated cheese

US: 4 bell peppers, 1 cup cooked rice, ½ cup black beans, ¼ cup sweetcorn

Instructions:

1. Stuff the peppers with a mixture of rice, beans, sweetcorn, and paprika.

2. Bake in the air fryer using the Bake function at 180°C (355°F) for 15-20 minutes.

3. Top with cheese and bake for another 2 minutes until melted. A dish with layers of deception!

Nutritional Info: Calories: 220 | Fat: 8g | Carbs: 30g | Protein: 8g

CHAPTER 3: DINNER TO DIE FOR

ONE-POT PRISON BREAK PASTA

Prep: 10 mins | Cook: 20 mins | Serves: 4
Cooking Function: Boil
Ingredients:

UK: 300g penne pasta, 400g diced tomatoes (canned), 200g chicken breast (diced), 1 onion (chopped), 2 garlic cloves (minced), 1 teaspoon dried oregano, 1 tablespoon olive oil, salt, pepper, grated Parmesan (for serving)

US: 10.5oz penne pasta, 14oz diced tomatoes (canned), 7oz chicken breast (diced), 1 onion (chopped), 2 garlic cloves (minced), 1 teaspoon dried oregano, 1 tablespoon olive oil, salt, pepper, grated Parmesan (for serving)

Instructions:

1. In a large pot, heat the olive oil over medium heat.
2. Add the onion and garlic, sautéing until softened (about 3 minutes).
3. Toss in the diced chicken and cook until browned.
4. Stir in the canned tomatoes, oregano, salt, pepper, and 800ml water. Bring to a boil.
5. Add the penne pasta and cook for about 10-12 minutes, stirring occasionally, until al dente.
6. Serve the One-Pot Prison Break Pasta hot, topped with grated Parmesan. This dish makes for a quick and easy dinner in the campervan!

Nutritional Info: Calories: 450 | Fat: 15g | Carbs: 55g | Protein: 30g

LETHAL INJECTION LEMON CHICKEN

Prep: 15 mins | Cook: 30 mins | Serves: 4
Cooking Function: Roast
Ingredients:

UK: 4 chicken thighs, juice and zest of 1 lemon, 2 garlic cloves (minced), 30ml olive oil, 1 teaspoon dried thyme, salt, pepper

US: 4 chicken thighs, juice and zest of 1 lemon, 2 garlic cloves (minced), 1oz olive oil, 1 teaspoon dried thyme, salt, pepper

Instructions:

1. Preheat your oven to 200°C (400°F).

2. In a bowl, mix the lemon juice, zest, garlic, olive oil, thyme, salt, and pepper.

3. Add the chicken thighs to the bowl, coating them well in the marinade. Let it sit for at least 10 minutes.

4. Place the chicken in a roasting dish and pour any remaining marinade over the top.

5. Roast in the oven for about 25-30 minutes, or until the chicken is golden and cooked through.

6. Serve the Lethal Injection Lemon Chicken hot, with a side of steamed veggies. A zesty delight for your campervan meals!

Nutritional Info: Calories: 350 | Fat: 20g | Carbs: 5g | Protein: 35g

RIGOR MORTIS RISOTTO

Prep: 10 mins | Cook: 30 mins | Serves: 4

Cooking Function: Stew

Ingredients:

UK: 250g arborio rice, 1 onion (chopped), 2 garlic cloves (minced), 1L chicken stock, 100g peas (frozen), 50g Parmesan cheese (grated), 30ml olive oil, salt, pepper

US: 8.8oz arborio rice, 1 onion (chopped), 2 garlic cloves (minced), 4.2 cups chicken stock, 3.5oz peas (frozen), 1.8oz Parmesan cheese (grated), 1oz olive oil, salt, pepper

Instructions:

1. In a large pot, heat the olive oil over medium heat.

2. Add the onion and garlic, cooking until softened.

3. Stir in the arborio rice, coating it in the oil for about 2 minutes.

4. Gradually add the chicken stock, one ladle at a time, stirring frequently until absorbed.

5. Once the rice is creamy and al dente (about 20 minutes), mix in the peas and Parmesan.

6. Serve the Rigor Mortis Risotto warm, garnished with more cheese. A comforting dish perfect for a chilly evening in your campervan!

Nutritional Info: Calories: 400 | Fat: 15g | Carbs: 55g | Protein: 15g

LAST MEAL LASAGNA

Prep: 20 mins | Cook: 45 mins | Serves: 4
Cooking Function: Bake
Ingredients:

UK: 9 lasagna sheets, 400g minced beef, 400g chopped tomatoes (canned), 1 onion (chopped), 2 garlic cloves (minced), 200g ricotta cheese, 100g mozzarella cheese (grated), 1 teaspoon dried oregano, salt, pepper

US: 9 lasagna sheets, 14oz minced beef, 14oz chopped tomatoes (canned), 1 onion (chopped), 2 garlic cloves (minced), 7oz ricotta cheese, 3.5oz mozzarella cheese (grated), 1 teaspoon dried oregano, salt, pepper

Instructions:

1. Preheat your oven to 180°C (350°F).
2. In a pan, sauté the onion and garlic until soft. Add the minced beef and cook until browned.
3. Stir in the chopped tomatoes, oregano, salt, and pepper, simmering for 10 minutes.
4. In a baking dish, layer the lasagna sheets, meat sauce, and ricotta. Repeat layers, finishing with meat sauce and topping with mozzarella.
5. Bake in the oven for 30-35 minutes until golden and bubbly.
6. Serve the Last Meal Lasagna hot, with a side salad. This hearty dish is sure to please any crowd on your camping trip!

Nutritional Info: Calories: 550 | Fat: 30g | Carbs: 40g | Protein: 35g

SHALLOW GRAVE SHEPHERD'S PIE

Prep: 15 mins | Cook: 45 mins | Serves: 4
Cooking Function: Bake
Ingredients:

UK: 500g minced lamb, 1 onion (chopped), 2 carrots (diced), 400g peas (frozen), 500g potatoes (peeled and chopped), 30ml milk, 50g butter, salt, pepper

US: 1.1lbs minced lamb, 1 onion (chopped), 2 carrots (diced), 14oz peas (frozen), 1.1lbs potatoes (peeled and chopped), 1oz milk, 1.8oz butter, salt, pepper

Instructions:

1. Preheat your oven to 200°C (400°F).
2. In a pan, cook the minced lamb with the onion and carrots until browned. Add the peas and season with salt and pepper.
3. Boil the potatoes in salted water until tender, then drain and mash with milk and butter.
4. Spread the lamb mixture in a baking dish and top with the mashed potatoes.
5. Bake for 25-30 minutes until the top is golden.
6. Serve the Shallow Grave Shepherd's Pie hot, a classic dish perfect for any campervan feast!

Nutritional Info: Calories: 500 | Fat: 25g | Carbs: 40g | Protein: 35g

ARSENIC AND OLD LACE CASSEROLE

Prep: 20 mins | Cook: 50 mins | Serves: 4

Cooking Function: Bake

Ingredients:

UK: 300g rice, 400g chicken (diced), 1 onion (chopped), 1 bell pepper (chopped), 1 can (400g) mushroom soup, 200ml chicken stock, salt, pepper, parsley (for garnish)

US: 10.5oz rice, 14oz chicken (diced), 1 onion (chopped), 1 bell pepper (chopped), 14oz mushroom soup, 0.8 cups chicken stock, salt, pepper, parsley (for garnish)

Instructions:

1. Preheat your oven to 180°C (350°F).
2. In a large bowl, combine all the ingredients except for the parsley. Mix well.
3. Transfer the mixture to a baking dish and cover with foil.
4. Bake for 40-45 minutes, stirring halfway through, until the chicken is cooked through.
5. Serve the Arsenic and Old Lace Casserole warm, garnished with parsley. A comforting and creamy delight for your campervan meals!

Nutritional Info: Calories: 450 | Fat: 15g | Carbs: 50g | Protein: 30g

HANGING JUDGE HALLOUMI SKEWERS

Prep: 10 mins | Cook: 15 mins | Serves: 4
Cooking Function: Grill
Ingredients:

UK: 300g halloumi cheese (cubed), 1 courgette (sliced), 1 bell pepper (chopped), 1 red onion (chopped), 30ml olive oil, 1 teaspoon dried oregano, salt, pepper

US: 10.5oz halloumi cheese (cubed), 1 courgette (sliced), 1 bell pepper (chopped), 1 red onion (chopped), 1oz olive oil, 1 teaspoon dried oregano, salt, pepper

Instructions:

1. Preheat your grill to medium-high.
2. In a bowl, mix the olive oil, oregano, salt, and pepper.
3. Toss the halloumi, courgette, bell pepper, and onion in the marinade.
4. Thread the vegetables and halloumi onto skewers.
5. Grill for about 10-15 minutes, turning occasionally, until the halloumi is golden and the veggies are tender.
6. Serve the Hanging Judge Halloumi Skewers hot, perfect for a quick and tasty meal on the go!

Nutritional Info: Calories: 300 | Fat: 22g | Carbs: 10g | Protein: 18g

DEATH ROW RATATOUILLE

Prep: 15 mins | Cook: 45 mins | Serves: 4
Cooking Function: Roast
Ingredients:

UK: 1 aubergine (diced), 2 courgettes (sliced), 1 bell pepper (chopped), 1 onion (chopped), 2 garlic cloves (minced), 400g chopped tomatoes (canned), 30ml olive oil, salt, pepper, basil (for garnish)

US: 1 eggplant (diced), 2 zucchinis (sliced), 1 bell pepper (chopped), 1 onion (chopped), 2 garlic cloves (minced), 14oz chopped tomatoes (canned), 1oz olive oil, salt, pepper, basil (for garnish)

Instructions:

1. Preheat your oven to 200°C (400°F).
2. In a large baking dish, combine all the chopped vegetables, garlic, chopped tomatoes, olive oil, salt, and pepper.
3. Toss well to coat the vegetables evenly.
4. Roast in the oven for about 35-40 minutes, stirring halfway through, until the vegetables are tender.
5. Serve the Death Row Ratatouille hot, garnished with fresh basil. A delicious vegetarian option for your campervan dinner!

Nutritional Info: Calories: 250 | Fat: 10g | Carbs: 35g | Protein: 5g

CEMENT SHOES SEAFOOD STEW

Prep: 15 mins | Cook: 30 mins | Serves: 4

Cooking Function: Stew

Ingredients:

UK: 300g mixed seafood (prawns, mussels, calamari), 1 onion (chopped), 2 garlic cloves (minced), 400g diced tomatoes (canned), 200ml fish stock, 1 teaspoon dried thyme, 30ml olive oil, salt, pepper, parsley (for garnish)

US: 10.5oz mixed seafood (prawns, mussels, calamari), 1 onion (chopped), 2 garlic cloves (minced), 14oz diced tomatoes (canned), 0.8 cups fish stock, 1 teaspoon dried thyme, 1oz olive oil, salt, pepper, parsley (for garnish)

Instructions:

1. In a large pot, heat the olive oil over medium heat.
2. Sauté the onion and garlic until softened.
3. Stir in the diced tomatoes, fish stock, thyme, salt, and pepper. Bring to a simmer.
4. Add the mixed seafood and cook for about 10 minutes until everything is cooked through.
5. Serve the Cement Shoes Seafood Stew hot, garnished with parsley. A hearty and flavorful meal for any seafood lover!

Nutritional Info: Calories: 300 | Fat: 15g | Carbs: 10g | Protein: 25g

MOB BOSS MEATBALLS

Prep: 15 mins | Cook: 25 mins | Serves: 4

Cooking Function: Bake

Ingredients:

UK: 500g minced beef, 1 egg, 100g breadcrumbs, 1 onion (finely chopped), 2 garlic cloves (minced), 1 teaspoon dried oregano, 30ml milk, salt, pepper, 400g tomato sauce (canned)

US: 1.1lbs minced beef, 1 egg, 3.5oz breadcrumbs, 1 onion (finely chopped), 2 garlic cloves (minced), 1 teaspoon dried oregano, 1oz milk, salt, pepper, 14oz tomato sauce (canned)

Instructions:

1. Preheat your oven to 200°C (400°F).

2. In a bowl, mix the minced beef, egg, breadcrumbs, onion, garlic, oregano, milk, salt, and pepper until well combined.

3. Form the mixture into meatballs and place them on a baking tray.

4. Bake in the oven for about 20-25 minutes until browned and cooked through.

5. Serve the Mob Boss Meatballs with tomato sauce over pasta or in a sub. A hearty dish fit for any mobster!

Nutritional Info: Calories: 400 | Fat: 25g | Carbs: 20g | Protein: 30g

PENAL CODE PESTO SALMON

Prep: 10 mins | Cook: 15 mins | Serves: 4

Cooking Function: Grill

Ingredients:

UK: 4 salmon fillets, 100g pesto (store-bought or homemade), 30ml olive oil, salt, pepper, lemon wedges (for serving)

US: 4 salmon fillets, 3.5oz pesto (store-bought or homemade), 1oz olive oil, salt, pepper, lemon wedges (for serving)

Instructions:

1. Preheat your grill to medium-high heat.
2. Brush the salmon fillets with olive oil, then season with salt and pepper.
3. Spread a generous layer of pesto over the top of each fillet.
4. Grill the salmon for about 10-12 minutes until it flakes easily with a fork.
5. Serve the Penal Code Pesto Salmon hot with lemon wedges on the side. A simple yet elegant dish perfect for any occasion!

Nutritional Info: Calories: 350 | Fat: 25g | Carbs: 5g | Protein: 30g

HOMICIDE DETECTIVE'S HOTPOT

Prep: 15 mins | Cook: 2 hours | Serves: 4

Cooking Function: Slow Cook

Ingredients:

UK: 500g beef stew meat, 2 potatoes (peeled and diced), 2 carrots (sliced), 1 onion (chopped), 2 garlic cloves (minced), 1L beef stock, 1 tablespoon Worcestershire sauce, salt, pepper, herbs de Provence

US: 1.1lbs beef stew meat, 2 potatoes (peeled and diced), 2 carrots (sliced), 1 onion (chopped), 2 garlic cloves (minced), 4.2 cups beef stock, 1 tablespoon Worcestershire sauce, salt, pepper, herbs de Provence

Instructions:

1. In a slow cooker, combine all the ingredients: beef, potatoes, carrots, onion, garlic, beef stock, Worcestershire sauce, salt, pepper, and herbs.
2. Stir everything well to ensure it's mixed.
3. Cover and cook on low for about 2 hours or until the beef is tender.
4. Serve the Homicide Detective's Hotpot hot, with crusty bread for dipping. A perfect meal for a chilly evening in your campervan!

Nutritional Info: Calories: 500 | Fat: 20g | Carbs: 40g | Protein: 40g

FORENSIC FILES FAJITAS

Prep: 15 mins | Cook: 15 mins | Serves: 4

Cooking Function: Sauté

Ingredients:

UK: 400g chicken breast (sliced), 1 bell pepper (sliced), 1 onion (sliced), 2 garlic cloves (minced), 2 teaspoons paprika, 30ml olive oil, salt, pepper, tortillas (to serve), sour cream (optional)

US: 14oz chicken breast (sliced), 1 bell pepper (sliced), 1 onion (sliced), 2 garlic cloves (minced), 2 teaspoons paprika, 1oz olive oil, salt, pepper, tortillas (to serve), sour cream (optional)

Instructions:

1. In a large pan, heat the olive oil over medium-high heat.

2. Add the chicken and cook until browned.

3. Toss in the bell pepper, onion, garlic, paprika, salt, and pepper, sautéing for another 5-7 minutes until the veggies are tender.

4. Serve the Forensic Files Fajitas in warm tortillas with sour cream if desired. A deliciously satisfying meal for any campervan adventure!

Nutritional Info: Calories: 450 | Fat: 15g | Carbs: 40g | Protein: 40g

CHAPTER 4: SINISTER SIDE DISHES

FINGERPRINT FOCACCIA

Prep: 10 mins | **Cook:** 20 mins | **Serves:** 6
Cooking Function: Air Fryer Bake
Ingredients:

UK: 500g strong white bread flour, 10g salt, 10g sugar, 7g instant yeast, 300ml warm water, 50ml olive oil, sea salt, rosemary (for topping)

US: 4 cups strong white bread flour, 1 teaspoon salt, 1 teaspoon sugar, 2¼ teaspoons instant yeast, 1¼ cups warm water, ¼ cup olive oil, sea salt, rosemary

Instructions:

1. In a large bowl, combine flour, salt, sugar, and yeast. Make a well in the centre and pour in warm water and olive oil.
2. Mix until a dough forms, then knead on a floured surface for about 5 minutes until smooth.
3. Place the dough in a lightly oiled bowl, cover, and let it rise in a warm spot for 1 hour or until doubled in size.
4. Preheat the air fryer to 200°C (400°F).
5. Once risen, flatten the dough onto a parchment-lined air fryer basket. Dimple the surface with your fingers.
6. Drizzle with olive oil, sprinkle with sea salt and rosemary, and bake for 15-20 minutes until golden.
7. Let cool slightly before slicing and serving this delicious focaccia alongside your main dishes.

Nutritional Info: Calories: 200 | Fat: 8g | Carbs: 30g | Protein: 6g

BALLISTICS REPORT BROCCOLI SALAD

Prep: 15 mins | **Cook:** 5 mins | **Serves:** 4
Cooking Function: Air Fryer Crisp
Ingredients:

UK: 300g broccoli florets, 50g feta cheese (crumbled), 30ml olive oil, 1 tablespoon lemon juice, salt, pepper, 30g sunflower seeds

US: 10.5oz broccoli florets, 1.75oz feta cheese, 2 tablespoons olive oil, 1 tablespoon lemon juice, salt, pepper, 1oz sunflower seeds

Instructions:

1. Preheat your air fryer to 200°C (400°F).

2. In a bowl, toss the broccoli florets with olive oil, lemon juice, salt, and pepper.

3. Place the broccoli in the air fryer basket and crisp for about 5 minutes until bright green and slightly charred.

4. Remove the broccoli and transfer to a serving bowl; top with crumbled feta and sunflower seeds. Serve this crunchy salad chilled or at room temperature for a side that makes a statement!

Nutritional Info: Calories: 180 | Fat: 14g | Carbs: 9g | Protein: 7g

CONSPIRACY THEORY COLESLAW

Prep: 10 mins | Cook: 0 mins | Serves: 6

Cooking Function: N/A

Ingredients:

UK: 300g white cabbage (finely shredded), 100g carrots (grated), 50g mayonnaise, 20ml apple cider vinegar, 1 tablespoon sugar, salt, pepper

US: 10.5oz white cabbage, 3.5oz carrots, 3.5oz mayonnaise, 1.5 tablespoons apple cider vinegar, 1 tablespoon sugar, salt, pepper

Instructions:

1. In a large bowl, combine the shredded cabbage and grated carrots.

2. In a separate bowl, mix mayonnaise, apple cider vinegar, sugar, salt, and pepper to create a dressing.

3. Pour the dressing over the cabbage and carrots, then toss well to coat.

4. Chill in the fridge for at least 30 minutes before serving for flavours that will keep you guessing!

Nutritional Info: Calories: 150 | Fat: 10g | Carbs: 12g | Protein: 2g

CHALK OUTLINE CAULIFLOWER

Prep: 10 mins | Cook: 20 mins | Serves: 4

Cooking Function: Air Fryer Roast

Ingredients:

UK: 1 head of cauliflower (cut into florets), 30ml olive oil, 1 teaspoon paprika, 1 teaspoon garlic powder, salt, pepper

US: 1 cauliflower head, 2 tablespoons olive oil, 1 teaspoon paprika, 1 teaspoon garlic powder, salt, pepper

Instructions:

1. Preheat your air fryer to 200°C (400°F).
2. In a large bowl, toss the cauliflower florets with olive oil, paprika, garlic powder, salt, and pepper until evenly coated.
3. Place the florets in the air fryer basket and roast for 15-20 minutes until golden and crispy, shaking halfway through.
4. Serve this lively cauliflower dish as a side that will surely leave an impression!

Nutritional Info: Calories: 120 | Fat: 9g | Carbs: 8g | Protein: 3g

EYEWITNESS ACCOUNT GREEN BEANS

Prep: 5 mins | Cook: 15 mins | Serves: 4

Cooking Function: Air Fryer Steam

Ingredients:

UK: 400g green beans (trimmed), 30ml olive oil, 1 garlic clove (minced), salt, pepper, lemon zest (for garnish)

US: 14oz green beans, 2 tablespoons olive oil, 1 garlic clove, salt, pepper, lemon zest

Instructions:

1. Preheat your air fryer to 180°C (356°F).
2. Toss the green beans with olive oil, minced garlic, salt, and pepper in a bowl.
3. Place them in the air fryer basket and steam for about 12-15 minutes until tender.
4. Garnish with lemon zest before serving this green side that adds a pop of freshness to your meal!

Nutritional Info: Calories: 80 | Fat: 6g | Carbs: 8g | Protein: 2g

LINEUP POTATO WEDGES

Prep: 10 mins | Cook: 25 mins | Serves: 4

Cooking Function: Air Fryer Roast

Ingredients:

UK: 800g potatoes (cut into wedges), 30ml olive oil, 1 teaspoon smoked paprika, 1 teaspoon dried oregano, salt, pepper

US: 1.75lbs potatoes, 2 tablespoons olive oil, 1 teaspoon smoked paprika, 1 teaspoon dried oregano, salt, pepper

Instructions:

1. Preheat your air fryer to 200°C (400°F).
2. In a bowl, toss the potato wedges with olive oil, smoked paprika, oregano, salt, and pepper until well coated.
3. Place the wedges in the air fryer basket and roast for about 25 minutes, shaking halfway through until crispy.
4. Serve hot alongside your favourite dip for a perfect side to any meal that everyone will want to "line up" for!

Nutritional Info: Calories: 220 | Fat: 10g | Carbs: 32g | Protein: 4g

FORENSIC EVIDENCE FRIES

Prep: 10 mins | Cook: 20 mins | Serves: 4

Cooking Function: Air Fryer Crisp

Ingredients:

UK: 800g potatoes (cut into fries), 30ml olive oil, 1 teaspoon garlic powder, 1 teaspoon onion powder, salt, pepper

US: 1.75lbs potatoes, 2 tablespoons olive oil, 1 teaspoon garlic powder, 1 teaspoon onion powder, salt, pepper

Instructions:

1. Preheat your air fryer to 200°C (400°F).
2. Toss the fries with olive oil, garlic powder, onion powder, salt, and pepper in a bowl until well-mixed.
3. Place them in the air fryer basket and crisp for about 20 minutes, shaking halfway through.
4. Enjoy these crispy fries as a side that will keep your guests guessing!

Nutritional Info: Calories: 230 | Fat: 12g | Carbs: 30g | Protein: 3g

COLD TRAIL CUCUMBER SALAD

Prep: 10 mins | Cook: 0 mins | Serves: 4
Cooking Function: N/A
Ingredients:

UK: 300g cucumber (sliced), 100g cherry tomatoes (halved), 50g red onion (thinly sliced), 30ml olive oil, 15ml white wine vinegar, salt, pepper, fresh dill (for garnish)

US: 10.5oz cucumber, 3.5oz cherry tomatoes, 3.5oz red onion, 2 tablespoons olive oil, 1 tablespoon white wine vinegar

Instructions:

1. In a bowl, combine cucumber, cherry tomatoes, and red onion.
2. In another bowl, whisk together olive oil, vinegar, salt, and pepper.
3. Pour the dressing over the salad and toss gently to combine.
4. Chill in the fridge for at least 30 minutes before serving this refreshing side that's perfect for warm nights!

Nutritional Info: Calories: 70 | Fat: 5g | Carbs: 6g | Protein: 2g

STAKEOUT SWEET POTATO MASH

Prep: 10 mins | Cook: 30 mins | Serves: 4
Cooking Function: Air Fryer Steam
Ingredients:

UK: 800g sweet potatoes (peeled and cubed), 30ml olive oil, 30ml milk, salt, pepper, pinch of nutmeg

US: 1.75lbs sweet potatoes, 2 tablespoons olive oil, 2 tablespoons milk, salt, pepper, pinch of nutmeg

Instructions:

1. Preheat your air fryer to 180°C (356°F).
2. Steam the sweet potato cubes in the air fryer for about 25-30 minutes until tender.
3. Once cooked, mash them in a bowl with olive oil, milk, salt, pepper, and nutmeg until smooth.
4. Serve this creamy sweet potato mash as a side dish that will have everyone coming back for seconds!

Nutritional Info: Calories: 180 | Fat: 5g | Carbs: 30g | Protein: 4g

UNDERCOVER ONION RINGS

Prep: 10 mins | Cook: 15 mins | Serves: 4

Cooking Function: Air Fryer Crisp

Ingredients:

UK: 2 large onions (sliced into rings), 100g breadcrumbs, 50g flour, 1 egg (beaten), 30ml milk, salt, pepper

US: 2 large onions, 3.5oz breadcrumbs, 1.75oz flour, 1 egg, 2 tablespoons milk, salt, pepper

Instructions:

1. Preheat your air fryer to 200°C (400°F).
2. Dip each onion ring first in flour, then in beaten egg mixed with milk, and finally coat with breadcrumbs.
3. Arrange the coated rings in the air fryer basket in a single layer and cook for about 15 minutes until golden and crispy, flipping halfway through.
4. Serve these crunchy onion rings hot with your favourite dipping sauce for a side that's always a hit!

Nutritional Info: Calories: 220 | Fat: 10g | Carbs: 28g | Protein: 4g

PLANTED EVIDENCE PEA SALAD

Prep: 10 mins | Cook: 0 mins | Serves: 4

Cooking Function: N/A

Ingredients:

UK: 300g frozen peas (thawed), 100g feta cheese (crumbled), 30ml olive oil, 20ml lemon juice, salt, pepper, fresh mint (for garnish)

US: 10.5oz frozen peas, 3.5oz feta cheese, 2 tablespoons olive oil, 1 tablespoon lemon juice, salt, pepper

Instructions:

1. In a bowl, mix the thawed peas with crumbled feta cheese.
2. Drizzle with olive oil and lemon juice, then season with salt and pepper.
3. Toss gently to combine, and garnish with fresh mint before serving this vibrant salad that adds a pop of colour to any meal!

Nutritional Info: Calories: 140 | Fat: 10g | Carbs: 10g | Protein: 6g

WIRETAP WATERCRESS SALAD

Prep: 5 mins | Cook: 0 mins | Serves: 4

Cooking Function: N/A

Ingredients:

UK: 100g watercress, 200g cherry tomatoes (halved), 50g cucumber (sliced), 30ml olive oil, 15ml balsamic vinegar, salt, pepper

US: 3.5oz watercress, 7oz cherry tomatoes, 1.75oz cucumber, 2 tablespoons olive oil, 1 tablespoon balsamic vinegar

Instructions:

1. In a large bowl, combine the watercress, cherry tomatoes, and cucumber.
2. Drizzle with olive oil and balsamic vinegar, then season with salt and pepper.
3. Toss gently to coat and serve this fresh, peppery salad as a delightful side!

Nutritional Info: Calories: 60 | Fat: 4g | Carbs: 6g | Protein: 2g

BURIED SECRETS BAKED BEANS

Prep: 10 mins | Cook: 1 hour | Serves: 4

Cooking Function: Air Fryer Bake

Ingredients:

UK: 400g canned baked beans, 100g chopped bacon, 30g brown sugar, 30ml barbecue sauce, 1 teaspoon mustard, salt, pepper

US: 14oz canned baked beans, 3.5oz chopped bacon, 2 tablespoons brown sugar, 2 tablespoons barbecue sauce, 1 teaspoon mustard

Instructions:

1. Preheat your air fryer to 180°C (356°F).
2. In a bowl, mix the baked beans, chopped bacon, brown sugar, barbecue sauce, mustard, salt, and pepper.
3. Transfer the mixture to a baking dish that fits in your air fryer.
4. Bake for about 45 minutes until bubbly and caramelized, stirring halfway through.
5. Serve these hearty baked beans hot as a comforting side that will leave everyone guessing what your secret ingredient is!

Nutritional Info: Calories: 220 | Fat: 10g | Carbs: 30g | Protein: 6g

CHAPTER 5: DESSERTS TO DIE FOR

DEATH BY CHOCOLATE MOUSSE

Prep: 15 mins | Cook: 0 mins | Serves: 4

Cooking Function: N/A

Ingredients:

UK: 200g dark chocolate (minimum 70% cocoa), 300ml double cream, 2 large eggs (separated), 50g caster sugar, a pinch of salt

US: 7oz dark chocolate, 1.25 cups heavy cream, 2 large eggs, 1.75oz granulated sugar, a pinch of salt

Instructions:

1. Melt the dark chocolate in a heatproof bowl over simmering water, stirring until smooth.
2. In another bowl, whip the double cream until soft peaks form. Set aside.
3. In a separate bowl, whisk the egg whites and salt until they form stiff peaks. Gradually add the sugar and whisk until glossy.
4. Fold the melted chocolate into the whipped cream gently, then fold in the egg whites until fully combined.
5. Spoon the mousse into individual serving dishes and chill in the fridge for at least 2 hours before serving.
6. Enjoy this rich dessert that's perfect for any spooky gathering!

Nutritional Info: Calories: 450 | Fat: 36g | Carbs: 20g | Protein: 6g

CYANIDE SURPRISE CHEESECAKE (NO-BAKE)

Prep: 20 mins | Cook: 4 hours | Serves: 8

Cooking Function: N/A

Ingredients:

UK: 250g digestive biscuits (crumbled), 100g unsalted butter (melted), 400g cream cheese, 100g icing sugar, 200ml double cream, 2 teaspoons vanilla extract

US: 9oz digestive biscuits, 3.5oz unsalted butter, 14oz cream cheese, 3.5oz powdered sugar, 0.75 cup heavy cream, 2 teaspoons vanilla extract

Instructions:

1. Mix the crumbled digestive biscuits with melted butter and press into the bottom of a loose-bottomed cake tin to form a base.

2. In a bowl, beat together the cream cheese, icing sugar, double cream, and vanilla extract until smooth and thick.

3. Pour the mixture over the biscuit base and smooth the top with a spatula.

4. Chill in the fridge for at least 4 hours or until set.

5. Slice and serve, revealing the delicious surprise within!

Nutritional Info: Calories: 350 | Fat: 25g | Carbs: 28g | Protein: 6g

LAST GASP LEMON BARS

Prep: 15 mins | Cook: 25 mins | Serves: 12

Cooking Function: Air Fryer Bake

Ingredients:

UK: 150g shortbread biscuits (crumbled), 75g unsalted butter (melted), 200g granulated sugar, 3 large eggs, 100ml fresh lemon juice, zest of 2 lemons, 50g plain flour, icing sugar (for dusting)

US: 5oz shortbread cookies, 2.5oz unsalted butter, 7oz granulated sugar, 3 large eggs, 0.4 cups fresh lemon juice, zest of 2 lemons, 1.75oz all-purpose flour, powdered sugar for dusting

Instructions:

1. Preheat the air fryer to 160°C (320°F).

2. Mix the crumbled shortbread biscuits with melted butter and press into the base of a lined baking dish.

3. In a separate bowl, whisk together the sugar, eggs, lemon juice, lemon zest, and flour until smooth.

4. Pour the lemon filling over the biscuit base and place it in the air fryer. Cook for 20-25 minutes until just set.

5. Allow to cool, dust with icing sugar, and cut into bars. Serve these zesty treats that pack a punch!

Nutritional Info: Calories: 180 | Fat: 9g | Carbs: 25g | Protein: 3g

BURIED ALIVE BANANA PUDDING

Prep: 10 mins | Cook: 0 mins | Serves: 6
Cooking Function: N/A
Ingredients:

UK: 400g ripe bananas (sliced), 300ml double cream, 100g condensed milk, 1 teaspoon vanilla extract, 200g vanilla wafers

US: 14oz ripe bananas, 1.25 cups heavy cream, 3.5oz sweetened condensed milk, 1 teaspoon vanilla extract, 7oz vanilla wafers

Instructions:

1. In a bowl, whip the double cream until soft peaks form, then mix in the condensed milk and vanilla extract.
2. In serving glasses, layer the sliced bananas, vanilla wafers, and cream mixture alternately.
3. Top with additional banana slices for decoration. Chill in the fridge for at least an hour before serving.
4. Enjoy this delightful and creamy dessert that's sure to please!

Nutritional Info: Calories: 320 | Fat: 18g | Carbs: 38g | Protein: 4g

CRIME SCENE CRUMBLE

Prep: 15 mins | Cook: 30 mins | Serves: 6
Cooking Function: Air Fryer Bake
Ingredients:

UK: 500g mixed berries (frozen), 150g oats, 100g plain flour, 100g brown sugar, 100g unsalted butter (cubed), pinch of salt

US: 17.5oz mixed berries, 5.5oz oats, 3.5oz all-purpose flour, 3.5oz brown sugar, 3.5oz unsalted butter, a pinch of salt

Instructions:

1. Preheat the air fryer to 180°C (356°F).
2. In a bowl, mix the frozen berries with half the brown sugar. Pour into a baking dish suitable for the air fryer.
3. In another bowl, combine oats, flour, remaining sugar, and butter until crumbly.
4. Sprinkle the crumble mixture over the berries and air fry for 25-30 minutes until golden and bubbly.
5. Serve this warm crumble with ice cream for a dessert that's truly criminal!

Nutritional Info: Calories: 250 | Fat: 10g | Carbs: 35g | Protein: 4g

POISONED APPLE PIE

Prep: 20 mins | Cook: 1 hour | Serves: 8

Cooking Function: Air Fryer Bake

Ingredients:

UK: 500g shortcrust pastry, 800g cooking apples (peeled and sliced), 100g sugar, 1 teaspoon cinnamon, 30g butter (dotted), 1 egg (for glazing)

US: 17.5oz shortcrust pastry, 28oz cooking apples, 3.5oz sugar, 1 teaspoon cinnamon, 1oz butter, 1 egg

Instructions:

1. Preheat the air fryer to 180°C (356°F).
2. Roll out the shortcrust pastry and line a pie dish, leaving some overhang for the top.
3. In a bowl, mix the sliced apples with sugar and cinnamon, then fill the pastry case with the mixture. Dot with butter.
4. Cover with remaining pastry, seal the edges, and make slits in the top for steam to escape.
5. Brush with beaten egg for a golden finish. Air fry for 50-60 minutes until golden brown and apples are tender.
6. Serve this delightful pie warm, and watch out for the extra kick!

Nutritional Info: Calories: 320 | Fat: 15g | Carbs: 45g | Protein: 4g

CORPUS DELICTI COOKIES

Prep: 15 mins | Cook: 10 mins | Serves: 12

Cooking Function: Air Fryer Bake

Ingredients:

UK: 200g butter (softened), 150g sugar, 1 large egg, 300g plain flour, 100g chocolate chips, pinch of salt

US: 7oz butter, 5.5oz sugar, 1 large egg, 10.5oz all-purpose flour, 3.5oz chocolate chips, a pinch of salt

Instructions:

1. In a bowl, cream together the softened butter and sugar until light and fluffy.
2. Beat in the egg until well combined.
3. Stir in the flour, chocolate chips, and salt until a dough forms.
4. Roll into balls and place them on a baking tray lined with parchment paper.
5. Air fry at 180°C (356°F) for about 8-10 minutes until lightly golden.
6. Let them cool and enjoy these delightful cookies that disappear faster than a corpse!

Nutritional Info: Calories: 150 | Fat: 8g | Carbs: 18g | Protein: 2g

DEADLY NIGHTSHADE BERRY PARFAIT

Prep: 10 mins | Cook: 0 mins | Serves: 4
Cooking Function: N/A

Ingredients:

UK: 200g blackberries, 200g blueberries, 300ml Greek yoghurt, 50g honey, mint leaves (for garnish)

US: 7oz blackberries, 7oz blueberries, 1.25 cups Greek yoghurt, 1.75oz honey, mint leaves for garnish

Instructions:

1. In serving glasses, layer the Greek yoghurt, mixed berries, and honey.
2. Repeat the layers until the glasses are full.
3. Garnish with mint leaves and serve immediately for a refreshing dessert that's dangerously delicious!

Nutritional Info: Calories: 220 | Fat: 5g | Carbs: 30g | Protein: 10g

SHALLOW GRAVE S'MORES

Prep: 10 mins | Cook: 5 mins | Serves: 4
Cooking Function: Air Fryer Bake

Ingredients:

UK: 8 digestive biscuits, 4 marshmallows, 100g milk chocolate, a pinch of salt
US: 8 digestive cookies, 4 marshmallows, 3.5oz milk chocolate, a pinch of salt

Instructions:

1. Lay out half the digestive biscuits on a baking tray.
2. Place a piece of chocolate and a marshmallow on each biscuit.
3. Top with the remaining biscuits to make sandwiches.
4. Air fry at 180°C (356°F) for about 5 minutes until the marshmallows are gooey.
5. Allow to cool slightly, then dig in for a sweet treat that's worth the grave!

Nutritional Info: Calories: 200 | Fat: 10g | Carbs: 26g | Protein: 2g

RIGOR MORTIS RICE PUDDING

Prep: 10 mins | Cook: 40 mins | Serves: 4

Cooking Function: Air Fryer Bake

Ingredients:

UK: 150g arborio rice, 500ml milk, 50g sugar, 1 teaspoon vanilla extract, cinnamon (for garnish)

US: 5.5oz arborio rice, 2 cups milk, 1.75oz sugar, 1 teaspoon vanilla extract, cinnamon for garnish

Instructions:

1. In a bowl, combine the rice, milk, sugar, and vanilla extract.
2. Pour the mixture into a baking dish suitable for the air fryer.
3. Air fry at 160°C (320°F) for 30-40 minutes, stirring occasionally until thickened.
4. Serve warm with a sprinkle of cinnamon on top for a comforting dessert!

Nutritional Info: Calories: 220 | Fat: 5g | Carbs: 40g | Protein: 5g

LETHAL INJECTION LAVA CAKE

Prep: 20 mins | Cook: 12 mins | Serves: 4

Cooking Function: Air Fryer Bake

Ingredients:

UK: 100g dark chocolate, 100g unsalted butter, 2 large eggs, 50g caster sugar, 40g plain flour

US: 3.5oz dark chocolate, 3.5oz unsalted butter, 2 large eggs, 1.75oz granulated sugar, 1.4oz all-purpose flour

Instructions:

1. Preheat the air fryer to 180°C (356°F).
2. Melt the chocolate and butter together in a heatproof bowl.
3. In a separate bowl, whisk the eggs and sugar until light and fluffy.
4. Fold in the melted chocolate mixture, then sift in the flour and gently fold until combined.
5. Pour the batter into greased ramekins and air fry for about 10-12 minutes until the edges are set but the centre is still gooey.
6. Let them sit for a minute, then turn them out onto plates. Cut into the centre to reveal the molten lava. Enjoy!

Nutritional Info: Calories: 320 | Fat: 20g | Carbs: 30g | Protein: 6g

COLD CASE COCONUT MACAROONS

Prep: 10 mins | Cook: 15 mins | Serves: 12

Cooking Function: Air Fryer Bake

Ingredients:

UK: 200g desiccated coconut, 2 large egg whites, 100g sugar, 1 teaspoon vanilla extract, pinch of salt

US: 7oz shredded coconut, 2 large egg whites, 3.5oz sugar, 1 teaspoon vanilla extract, pinch of salt

Instructions:

1. In a bowl, mix the desiccated coconut, egg whites, sugar, vanilla extract, and salt until combined.
2. Scoop tablespoon-sized balls of the mixture and place them on a lined baking tray.
3. Air fry at 160°C (320°F) for 12-15 minutes until golden.
4. Allow to cool before serving these delightful treats that'll leave you wanting more!

Nutritional Info: Calories: 150 | Fat: 5g | Carbs: 22g | Protein: 2g

AUTOPSY REPORT AFFOGATO

Prep: 5 mins | Cook: 0 mins | Serves: 2

Cooking Function: N/A

Ingredients:

UK: 2 scoops vanilla ice cream, 2 shots espresso (or strong coffee), cocoa powder (for dusting)

US: 2 scoops vanilla ice cream, 2 shots espresso, cocoa powder for dusting

Instructions:

1. Place a scoop of vanilla ice cream in each serving glass.

2. Brew the espresso and pour over the ice cream.

3. Dust with cocoa powder and serve immediately for a quick and delicious treat that'll give you chills!

Nutritional Info: Calories: 220 | Fat: 10g | Carbs: 30g | Protein: 4g

CHAPTER 6: MYSTERIOUS MUNCHIES AND SNACKS

STAKE-OUT SPICED NUTS

Prep: 10 mins | Cook: 15 mins | Serves: 4

Cooking Function: Air Fryer Roast

Ingredients:

UK: 200g mixed nuts (almonds, cashews, pecans), 15ml olive oil, 1 teaspoon smoked paprika, 1 teaspoon garlic powder, 1 teaspoon cayenne pepper, salt to taste

US: 7oz mixed nuts (almonds, cashews, pecans), 1 tablespoon olive oil, 1 teaspoon smoked paprika, 1 teaspoon garlic powder, 1 teaspoon cayenne pepper, salt to taste

Instructions:

1. Preheat your air fryer to 160°C (320°F).
2. In a mixing bowl, combine the mixed nuts, olive oil, smoked paprika, garlic powder, cayenne pepper, and a pinch of salt. Toss until the nuts are well coated.
3. Spread the nuts evenly in the air fryer basket.
4. Air fry for about 10-15 minutes, shaking the basket halfway through until the nuts are golden and fragrant.
5. Allow to cool slightly before serving as a deliciously crunchy snack perfect for any stakeout!

Nutritional Info: Calories: 180 | Fat: 15g | Carbs: 8g | Protein: 6g

CONFIDENTIAL INFORMANT CHEESE DIP

Prep: 5 mins | Cook: 10 mins | Serves: 4

Cooking Function: Air Fryer Bake

Ingredients:

UK: 200g cream cheese, 100g sour cream, 150g grated cheddar cheese, 50g grated mozzarella cheese, 1 tablespoon hot sauce, salt and pepper to taste

US: 7oz cream cheese, 3.5oz sour cream, 5oz grated cheddar cheese, 1.75oz grated mozzarella cheese, 1 tablespoon hot sauce, salt and pepper to taste

Instructions:

1. In a mixing bowl, combine cream cheese, sour cream, cheddar cheese, mozzarella cheese, hot sauce, salt, and pepper. Mix until smooth.
2. Transfer the mixture to a baking dish suitable for the air fryer.
3. Air fry at 180°C (356°F) for 8-10 minutes until bubbly and golden on top.
4. Serve hot with tortilla chips or fresh veggies for a cheesy delight that's undercover delicious!

Nutritional Info: Calories: 250 | Fat: 20g | Carbs: 8g | Protein: 10g

PLANTED EVIDENCE POPCORN

Prep: 5 mins | Cook: 5 mins | Serves: 2

Cooking Function: Air Fryer Popcorn

Ingredients:

UK: 100g popcorn kernels, 15ml coconut oil, 1 teaspoon sea salt, 1 teaspoon nutritional yeast (optional)

US: 3.5oz popcorn kernels, 1 tablespoon coconut oil, 1 teaspoon sea salt, 1 teaspoon nutritional yeast (optional)

Instructions:

1. Preheat your air fryer to 200°C (392°F).
2. In a bowl, combine the popcorn kernels with coconut oil and salt. Toss well to coat.
3. Place the kernels in the air fryer basket in a single layer.
4. Air fry for about 4-5 minutes, shaking the basket every couple of minutes until popping slows down.
5. Once done, sprinkle with nutritional yeast for a cheesy flavour if desired. Enjoy your "evidence" with a movie!

Nutritional Info: Calories: 120 | Fat: 7g | Carbs: 14g | Protein: 3g

WIRETAP WONTONS

Prep: 20 mins | Cook: 10 mins | Serves: 6

Cooking Function: Air Fryer Crisp

Ingredients:

UK: 200g minced pork, 100g chopped spring onions, 1 tablespoon soy sauce, 1 teaspoon sesame oil, 30 wonton wrappers, sweet chilli sauce (for dipping)

US: 7oz minced pork, 3.5oz chopped green onions, 1 tablespoon soy sauce, 1 teaspoon sesame oil, 30 wonton wrappers, sweet chilli sauce for dipping

Instructions:

1. In a bowl, mix minced pork, spring onions, soy sauce, and sesame oil until well combined.
2. Place a teaspoon of the filling in the centre of each wonton wrapper.
3. Fold the wrapper over to form a triangle and pinch the edges to seal.
4. Lightly spray the air fryer basket with oil and arrange the wontons in a single layer.
5. Air fry at 180°C (356°F) for 8-10 minutes until golden and crispy. Serve with sweet chilli sauce for a thrilling snack!

Nutritional Info: Calories: 150 | Fat: 8g | Carbs: 12g | Protein: 10g

COLD TRAIL CRUDITÉS

Prep: 10 mins | Cook: 0 mins | Serves: 4

Cooking Function: N/A

Ingredients:

UK: 100g carrot sticks, 100g cucumber sticks, 100g bell pepper slices, 50g cherry tomatoes, 100g hummus (for dipping)

US: 3.5oz carrot sticks, 3.5oz cucumber sticks, 3.5oz bell pepper slices, 3.5oz cherry tomatoes, 3.5oz hummus for dipping

Instructions:

1. Arrange the carrot sticks, cucumber sticks, bell pepper slices, and cherry tomatoes on a serving platter.
2. Serve with a bowl of hummus in the centre for dipping.
3. Enjoy this healthy and refreshing snack while discussing your latest "case" with friends!

Nutritional Info: Calories: 120 | Fat: 5g | Carbs: 15g | Protein: 3g

UNDERCOVER HUMMUS

Prep: 5 mins | Cook: 0 mins | Serves: 4

Cooking Function: N/A

Ingredients:

UK: 400g canned chickpeas (drained), 30ml tahini, 30ml olive oil, 1 garlic clove (minced), juice of 1 lemon, salt to taste, water as needed

US: 14oz canned chickpeas (drained), 2 tablespoons tahini, 2 tablespoons olive oil, 1 garlic clove minced, juice of 1 lemon, salt to taste, water as needed

Instructions:

1. In a food processor, combine chickpeas, tahini, olive oil, minced garlic, lemon juice, and salt. Blend until smooth.

2. Add water a tablespoon at a time until you reach your desired consistency.

3. Transfer to a bowl and serve with pita chips or fresh veggies for an undercover snack that's always a hit!

Nutritional Info: Calories: 150 | Fat: 10g | Carbs: 15g | Protein: 6g

GETAWAY VEHICLE GUACAMOLE

Prep: 5 mins | Cook: 0 mins | Serves: 2

Cooking Function: N/A

Ingredients:

UK: 2 ripe avocados, juice of 1 lime, 1 small red onion (finely chopped), 1 small tomato (diced), salt to taste, chopped coriander (for garnish)

US: 2 ripe avocados, juice of 1 lime, 1 small red onion (finely chopped), 1 small tomato (diced), salt to taste, chopped cilantro for garnish

Instructions:

1. In a bowl, mash the avocados with a fork.

2. Add lime juice, red onion, tomato, and salt. Mix until well combined.

3. Garnish with chopped coriander before serving with tortilla chips or fresh veggies. This guacamole will get you away in a flash!

Nutritional Info: Calories: 240 | Fat: 18g | Carbs: 12g | Protein: 3g

POWDER RESIDUE PARMESAN CRISPS

Prep: 5 mins | Cook: 10 mins | Serves: 4

Cooking Function: Air Fryer Crisp

Ingredients:

UK: 100g grated Parmesan cheese, 1 teaspoon garlic powder, 1 teaspoon paprika, pinch of black pepper

US: 3.5oz grated Parmesan cheese, 1 teaspoon garlic powder, 1 teaspoon paprika, pinch of black pepper

Instructions:

1. In a bowl, mix grated Parmesan, garlic powder, paprika, and black pepper until combined.
2. Place small mounds of the cheese mixture onto a baking tray lined with parchment paper, spacing them out.
3. Air fry at 200°C (392°F) for about 5-7 minutes until golden and crispy.
4. Let them cool before serving as perfect "evidence" for your next snack!

Nutritional Info: Calories: 130 | Fat: 10g | Carbs: 1g | Protein: 10g

LINEUP BRUSCHETTA

Prep: 10 mins | Cook: 5 mins | Serves: 6

Cooking Function: Air Fryer Toast

Ingredients:

UK: 1 baguette (sliced), 200g diced tomatoes, 1 garlic clove (minced), 30ml olive oil, 1 teaspoon balsamic vinegar, salt and pepper to taste, chopped basil for garnish

US: 1 baguette (sliced), 7oz diced tomatoes, 1 garlic clove (minced), 2 tablespoons olive oil, 1 teaspoon balsamic vinegar, salt and pepper to taste, chopped basil for garnish

Instructions:

1. In a bowl, mix diced tomatoes, minced garlic, olive oil, balsamic vinegar, salt, and pepper.
2. Spread the tomato mixture onto the baguette slices.
3. Air fry at 180°C (356°F) for about 5 minutes until the bread is toasted.
4. Garnish with chopped basil before serving for a delicious lineup of flavours!

Nutritional Info: Calories: 180 | Fat: 8g | Carbs: 25g | Protein: 4g

EYEWITNESS ACCOUNT EDAMAME

Prep: 5 mins | Cook: 5 mins | Serves: 2

Cooking Function: Air Fryer Steam

Ingredients:

UK: 200g edamame pods, 1 tablespoon soy sauce, 1 teaspoon sesame oil, salt to taste

US: 7oz edamame pods, 1 tablespoon soy sauce, 1 teaspoon sesame oil, salt to taste

Instructions:

1. Place edamame pods in the air fryer basket and steam at 160°C (320°F) for 4-5 minutes.
2. Once cooked, toss with soy sauce, sesame oil, and a pinch of salt.
3. Serve warm for a quick and healthy snack that's easy to enjoy while keeping an eye on the "situation"!

Nutritional Info: Calories: 120 | Fat: 5g | Carbs: 10g | Protein: 10g

BREAKING BREADSTICKS

Prep: 10 mins | Cook: 15 mins | Serves: 4

Cooking Function: Air Fryer Bake

Ingredients:

UK: 250g breadstick dough, 50g grated Parmesan cheese, 1 teaspoon garlic powder, 30ml olive oil, salt to taste

US: 9oz breadstick dough, 1.75oz grated Parmesan cheese, 1 teaspoon garlic powder, 2 tablespoons olive oil, salt to taste

Instructions:

1. Preheat your air fryer to 200°C (392°F).
2. Roll the breadstick dough into thin sticks and place them on a baking tray.
3. Brush with olive oil and sprinkle with Parmesan cheese, garlic powder, and salt.
4. Air fry for about 10-15 minutes until golden and crispy.
5. Serve warm for a fun snack that's perfect for a night in!

Nutritional Info: Calories: 220 | Fat: 10g | Carbs: 28g | Protein: 6g

MISDEMEANOR MOZZARELLA STICKS

Prep: 10 mins | Cook: 10 mins | Serves: 4

Cooking Function: Air Fryer Crisp

Ingredients:

UK: 200g mozzarella cheese (cut into sticks), 100g breadcrumbs, 1 egg (beaten), 50g flour, salt and pepper to taste

US: 7oz mozzarella cheese (cut into sticks), 3.5oz breadcrumbs, 1 egg (beaten), 1.75oz flour, salt and pepper to taste

Instructions:

1. Set up a breading station with three bowls: one for flour, one for the beaten egg, and one for breadcrumbs.
2. Dip each mozzarella stick into flour, then egg, and finally breadcrumbs. Ensure they're well coated.
3. Place the coated sticks in the air fryer basket.
4. Air fry at 180°C (356°F) for about 8-10 minutes until golden and melty.
5. Serve with marinara sauce for a snack that breaks the rules of deliciousness!

Nutritional Info: Calories: 300 | Fat: 20g | Carbs: 25g | Protein: 12g

PROBABLE CAUSE PITA CHIPS

Prep: 5 mins | Cook: 10 mins | Serves: 4

Cooking Function: Air Fryer Crisp

Ingredients:

UK: 4 pita bread, 30ml olive oil, 1 teaspoon garlic powder, 1 teaspoon paprika, salt to taste

US: 4 pita bread, 2 tablespoons olive oil, 1 teaspoon garlic powder, 1 teaspoon paprika, salt to taste

Instructions:

1. Preheat your air fryer to 200°C (392°F).
2. Cut the pita bread into triangles and place them in a bowl.
3. Drizzle with olive oil, garlic powder, paprika, and salt. Toss until coated.
4. Arrange the pita chips in the air fryer basket.
5. Air fry for about 8-10 minutes until golden and crisp. Serve with your favourite dip for a snack that's sure to be "probable" delicious!

Nutritional Info: Calories: 220 | Fat: 10g | Carbs: 30g | Protein: 6g

CHAPTER 7: DRINKS TO PUT YOU UNDER

BLOODY MURDER MARY

Prep: 10 mins | Cook: 0 mins | Serves: 2 glasses
Cooking Function: Blend
Ingredients:

UK: 400ml tomato juice, 50ml vodka, 2 teaspoons Worcestershire sauce, 1 teaspoon hot sauce, 1 teaspoon lemon juice, salt and pepper to taste, celery sticks and lemon wedges (for garnish)

US: 14oz tomato juice, 1.7oz vodka, 2 teaspoons Worcestershire sauce, 1 teaspoon hot sauce, 1 teaspoon lemon juice, salt and pepper to taste, celery sticks and lemon wedges (for garnish)

Instructions:

1. In a blender, combine the tomato juice, vodka, Worcestershire sauce, hot sauce, lemon juice, salt, and pepper.
2. Blend until well-mixed.
3. Taste and adjust seasoning if necessary; blend again to incorporate.
4. Pour the mixture into glasses filled with ice.
5. Garnish with celery sticks and lemon wedges before serving. Enjoy this "bloody" concoction that's perfect for any occasion!

Nutritional Info: Calories: 120 | Fat: 0g | Carbs: 8g | Protein: 3g

LONG ARM OF THE LAW LEMONADE

Prep: 5 mins | Cook: 0 mins | Serves: 4 glasses
Cooking Function: Mix
Ingredients:

UK: 250ml fresh lemon juice, 1 litre water, 200g sugar, ice cubes, lemon slices (for garnish)

US: 1 cup fresh lemon juice, 4 cups water, 1 cup sugar, ice cubes, lemon slices (for garnish)

Instructions:

1. In a pitcher, combine the fresh lemon juice, water, and sugar.
2. Stir well until the sugar dissolves completely.
3. Taste and adjust sweetness by adding more sugar if desired.
4. Chill in the fridge for at least 30 minutes.
5. Serve over ice and garnish with lemon slices. This lemonade will keep you refreshed while you're out on the open road!

Nutritional Info: Calories: 130 | Fat: 0g | Carbs: 34g | Protein: 0g

DEATH IN THE AFTERNOON ICED TEA

Prep: 5 mins | Cook: 10 mins | Serves: 2 glasses

Cooking Function: Brew

Ingredients:

UK: 2 bags of black tea, 300ml boiling water, 100ml gin, ice cubes, fresh mint leaves (for garnish)

US: 2 bags of black tea, 1.3 cups boiling water, 3.4oz gin, ice cubes, fresh mint leaves (for garnish)

Instructions:

1. Brew the black tea in boiling water for about 5-10 minutes, then remove the tea bags.

2. Allow the tea to cool down to room temperature.

3. In a glass, combine the cooled tea and gin over ice.

4. Stir gently and garnish with fresh mint leaves. Sip slowly and enjoy this chilling drink!

Nutritional Info: Calories: 220 | Fat: 0g | Carbs: 10g | Protein: 0g

STIFF AS A CORPSE COLD BREW

Prep: 5 mins | Cook: 12 hours | Serves: 4 glasses

Cooking Function: Brew

Ingredients:

UK: 100g coarsely ground coffee, 1 litre cold water, ice cubes, milk or cream (optional)

US: 3.5oz coarsely ground coffee, 4 cups cold water, ice cubes, milk or cream (optional)

Instructions:

1. In a large jar, combine the coarsely ground coffee and cold water.

2. Stir to ensure all coffee grounds are submerged.

3. Cover and steep in the fridge for 12 hours.

4. After steeping, strain the coffee using a fine mesh sieve or cheesecloth to remove the grounds.

5. Serve over ice and add milk or cream if desired. This cold brew will keep you alert while you're camping in the great outdoors!

Nutritional Info: Calories: 5 (without milk) | Fat: 0g | Carbs: 0g | Protein: 0g

SHALLOW GRAVE SMOOTHIE

Prep: 5 mins | Cook: 0 mins | Serves: 2 glasses

Cooking Function: Blend

Ingredients:

UK: 150g spinach, 1 banana, 200ml almond milk, 30g peanut butter, 1 tablespoon honey

US: 5oz spinach, 1 banana, 7oz almond milk, 1oz peanut butter, 1 tablespoon honey

Instructions:

1. In a blender, combine spinach, banana, almond milk, peanut butter, and honey.
2. Blend until smooth and creamy.
3. Taste and adjust sweetness with more honey if desired.
4. Pour into glasses and enjoy this nutrient-packed smoothie that's to die for!

Nutritional Info: Calories: 300 | Fat: 12g | Carbs: 38g | Protein: 10g

LAST MEAL MILKSHAKE

Prep: 5 mins | Cook: 0 mins | Serves: 2 glasses

Cooking Function: Blend

Ingredients:

UK: 300ml milk, 100g vanilla ice cream, 2 tablespoons chocolate syrup, 1 tablespoon crushed biscuits (for garnish)

US: 10oz milk, 3.5oz vanilla ice cream, 2 tablespoons chocolate syrup, 1 tablespoon crushed biscuits (for garnish)

Instructions:

1. In a blender, combine milk, vanilla ice cream, and chocolate syrup.
2. Blend until smooth and creamy.
3. Pour into glasses and top with crushed biscuits. This milkshake is the perfect indulgence for a sweet treat!

Nutritional Info: Calories: 400 | Fat: 18g | Carbs: 52g | Protein: 8g

DEADLY NIGHTCAP HOT CHOCOLATE

Prep: 5 mins | Cook: 10 mins | Serves: 2 mugs

Cooking Function: Heat

Ingredients:

UK: 500ml milk, 100g dark chocolate (chopped), 2 tablespoons sugar, whipped cream (for topping)

US: 17oz milk, 3.5oz dark chocolate (chopped), 2 tablespoons sugar, whipped cream (for topping)

Instructions:

1. In a saucepan, heat the milk over medium heat until it's hot but not boiling.
2. Stir in the chopped dark chocolate and sugar until melted and smooth.
3. Pour into mugs and top with whipped cream. Sip slowly and enjoy the warming sensation!

Nutritional Info: Calories: 350 | Fat: 20g | Carbs: 30g | Protein: 10g

POISONED CHALICE PUNCH

Prep: 15 mins | Cook: 0 mins | Serves: 6 glasses

Cooking Function: Mix

Ingredients:

UK: 1-litre cranberry juice, 500ml lemonade, 200ml vodka, fresh fruit slices (for garnish)

US: 34oz cranberry juice, 17oz lemonade, 7oz vodka, fresh fruit slices (for garnish)

Instructions:

1. In a large bowl or pitcher, combine cranberry juice, lemonade, and vodka.
2. Stir well to mix the ingredients thoroughly.
3. Chill in the fridge for about 30 minutes before serving.
4. Serve in glasses with fresh fruit slices as garnish. This punch is perfect for sharing!

Nutritional Info: Calories: 180 | Fat: 0g | Carbs: 25g | Protein: 0g

RIGOR MORTIS REFRESHER

Prep: 5 mins | Cook: 0 mins | Serves: 2 glasses

Cooking Function: Mix

Ingredients:

UK: 300ml coconut water, 100ml pineapple juice, 1 lime (juiced), ice cubes

US: 10oz coconut water, 3.4oz pineapple juice, 1 lime (juiced), ice cubes

Instructions:

1. In a shaker, combine coconut water, pineapple juice, and lime juice.
2. Shake well until mixed and chilled.
3. Pour over ice in glasses and enjoy this tropical refresher on your next adventure!

Nutritional Info: Calories: 70 | Fat: 0g | Carbs: 17g | Protein: 1g

CORPUS DELICTI COCKTAIL (NON-ALCOHOLIC)

Prep: 5 mins | Cook: 0 mins | Serves: 2 glasses

Cooking Function: Mix

Ingredients:

UK: 250ml pomegranate juice, 250ml soda water, 1 tablespoon lemon juice, ice cubes, mint leaves (for garnish)

US: 8.5oz pomegranate juice, 8.5oz soda water, 1 tablespoon lemon juice, ice cubes, mint leaves (for garnish)

Instructions:

1. In a pitcher, mix pomegranate juice, soda water, and lemon juice.
2. Stir gently to combine.
3. Pour over ice in glasses and garnish with mint leaves. Enjoy this refreshing non-alcoholic cocktail!

Nutritional Info: Calories: 60 | Fat: 0g | Carbs: 15g | Protein: 0g

CRIME SCENE CLEANER GREEN JUICE

Prep: 10 mins | Cook: 0 mins | Serves: 2 glasses

Cooking Function: Blend

Ingredients:

UK: 200g spinach, 1 cucumber, 1 green apple, 1 lemon (juiced), 250ml water

US: 7oz spinach, 1 cucumber, 1 green apple, 1 lemon (juiced), 1 cup water

Instructions:

1. In a blender, combine spinach, cucumber, green apple, lemon juice, and water.
2. Blend until smooth.
3. Strain through a fine sieve if desired for a smoother texture.
4. Serve over ice and enjoy this detoxifying drink!

Nutritional Info: Calories: 80 | Fat: 0g | Carbs: 20g | Protein: 3g

INTERROGATION ROOM ICED COFFEE

Prep: 5 mins | Cook: 0 mins | Serves: 2 glasses

Cooking Function: Brew

Ingredients:

UK: 250ml brewed coffee (cooled), 100ml milk, 2 tablespoons sugar, ice cubes

US: 8.5oz brewed coffee (cooled), 3.4oz milk, 2 tablespoons sugar, ice cubes

Instructions:

1. Brew your coffee and allow it to cool.
2. In a glass, combine cooled coffee, milk, and sugar.
3. Stir until the sugar dissolves.
4. Serve over ice and enjoy this energizing drink that'll keep you awake on the road!

Nutritional Info: Calories: 120 | Fat: 4g | Carbs: 18g | Protein: 3g

LETHAL INJECTION LATTE

Prep: 5 mins | Cook: 0 mins | Serves: 1 cup

Cooking Function: Brew

Ingredients:

UK: 150ml brewed espresso, 150ml steamed milk, 1 tablespoon vanilla syrup, cocoa powder (for garnish)

US: 5oz brewed espresso, 5oz steamed milk, 1 tablespoon vanilla syrup, cocoa powder (for garnish)

Instructions:

1. Brew the espresso and pour it into a cup.
2. Steam the milk and pour it over the espresso.
3. Stir in the vanilla syrup.
4. Garnish with a sprinkle of cocoa powder. Enjoy this delightful coffee concoction that's as good as it gets!

Nutritional Info: Calories: 200 | Fat: 7g | Carbs: 26g | Protein: 6g

CHAPTER 8: PRESERVED EVIDENCE (PICKLES AND PRESERVES)

CORPUS DELICTI CUCUMBER PICKLES

Prep: 15 mins | Cook: 0 mins | Serves: 4 jars
Cooking Function: No Cook
Ingredients:

UK: 1kg cucumbers (sliced), 500ml white vinegar, 200g granulated sugar, 50g salt, 2 teaspoons mustard seeds, 1 teaspoon black peppercorns, 2 teaspoons dill seeds, 4 cloves garlic (sliced)

US: 2.2lbs cucumbers (sliced), 2 cups white vinegar, 1 cup granulated sugar, 3.5oz salt, 2 teaspoons mustard seeds, 1 teaspoon black peppercorns, 2 teaspoons dill seeds, 4 cloves garlic (sliced)

Instructions:

1. In a large bowl, toss the cucumber slices with salt and let them sit for 10 minutes to draw out excess moisture.
2. In a saucepan, combine white vinegar, sugar, mustard seeds, black peppercorns, dill seeds, and garlic. Heat over medium until the sugar dissolves, then remove from heat.
3. Rinse the cucumbers and pack them tightly into sterilized jars.
4. Pour the vinegar mixture over the cucumbers, ensuring they're fully submerged.
5. Seal the jars and refrigerate for at least 24 hours before enjoying. Perfect for camping sandwiches or snacks on the road!

Nutritional Info: Calories: 50 | Fat: 0g | Carbs: 12g | Protein: 1g

BLOOD SPATTER BEETROOT CHUTNEY

Prep: 10 mins | Cook: 1 hour | Serves: 4 jars
Cooking Function: Slow Cook
Ingredients:

UK: 500g beetroot (peeled and chopped), 1 onion (finely chopped), 100g brown sugar, 250ml apple cider vinegar, 1 teaspoon ground ginger, 1 teaspoon mustard seeds, 1 teaspoon salt, 1/2 teaspoon black pepper

US: 1.1lbs beetroot (peeled and chopped), 1 onion (finely chopped), 1/2 cup brown sugar, 1 cup apple cider vinegar, 1 teaspoon ground ginger, 2 teaspoons mustard seeds, 1 teaspoon salt, 1/2 teaspoon black pepper

Instructions:

1. In a slow cooker, combine beetroot, onion, brown sugar, apple cider vinegar, ginger, mustard seeds, salt, and black pepper.

2. Stir well and cover the slow cooker. Cook on low for 1 hour, stirring occasionally.

3. Once thickened, allow to cool slightly before transferring to sterilized jars.

4. Seal and store in the fridge for up to 3 weeks. This tangy chutney is perfect with cheese or cold meats during your campervan adventures!

Nutritional Info: Calories: 70 | Fat: 0g | Carbs: 18g | Protein: 1g

BURIED BODY ONION JAM

Prep: 10 mins | Cook: 1 hour | Serves: 2 jars

Cooking Function: Slow Cook

Ingredients:

UK: 500g red onions (sliced), 100g brown sugar, 100ml balsamic vinegar, 1 teaspoon salt, 1/2 teaspoon black pepper, 1 tablespoon olive oil

US: 1.1lbs red onions (sliced), 1/2 cup brown sugar, 1/3 cup balsamic vinegar, 1 teaspoon salt, 1/2 teaspoon black pepper, 1 tablespoon olive oil

Instructions:

1. Heat olive oil in a frying pan over medium heat. Add sliced onions and cook for about 5 minutes until softened.

2. Stir in brown sugar, balsamic vinegar, salt, and pepper. Reduce heat to low and simmer for 45 minutes, stirring occasionally until thickened.

3. Let the onion jam cool, then transfer to sterilized jars and seal.

4. This sweet and savoury jam pairs perfectly with meats or as a gourmet addition to sandwiches during your travels!

Nutritional Info: Calories: 60 | Fat: 2g | Carbs: 14g | Protein: 1g

COLD CASE KIMCHI

Prep: 20 mins | Cook: 0 mins | Serves: 4 jars
Cooking Function: No Cook
Ingredients:

UK: 1kg napa cabbage (chopped), 150g sea salt, 3 cloves garlic (minced), 1 tablespoon ginger (grated), 2 tablespoons sugar, 2 tablespoons fish sauce (or soy sauce for a vegetarian version), 3 tablespoons Korean red pepper flakes

US: 2.2lbs napa cabbage (chopped), 5.5oz sea salt, 3 cloves garlic (minced), 1 tablespoon ginger (grated), 2 tablespoons sugar, 2 tablespoons fish sauce (or soy sauce), 3 tablespoons Korean red pepper flakes

Instructions:

1. In a large bowl, mix the chopped napa cabbage with sea salt and let it sit for 2 hours, turning occasionally.
2. In a separate bowl, combine garlic, ginger, sugar, fish sauce, and Korean red pepper flakes to form a paste.
3. After 2 hours, rinse the cabbage and drain well.
4. Mix the cabbage with the spice paste until well-coated.
5. Pack the mixture tightly into sterilized jars, leaving a little space at the top for fermentation.
6. Seal the jars and let them ferment at room temperature for 2-3 days before refrigerating. Enjoy this spicy condiment with your campervan meals!

Nutritional Info: Calories: 30 | Fat: 0g | Carbs: 6g | Protein: 1g

SHALLOW GRAVE SAUERKRAUT

Prep: 15 mins | Cook: 0 mins | Serves: 4 jars
Cooking Function: No Cook
Ingredients:

UK: 1kg green cabbage (finely shredded), 30g sea salt, 1 tablespoon caraway seeds

US: 2.2lbs green cabbage (finely shredded), 1oz sea salt, 1 tablespoon caraway seeds

Instructions:

1. In a large bowl, mix shredded cabbage and sea salt. Massage the cabbage for about 5 minutes until it begins to release its juices.
2. Add caraway seeds and mix well.
3. Pack the mixture tightly into sterilized jars, ensuring the liquid covers the cabbage completely.
4. Seal the jars and let them ferment at room temperature for 1-4 weeks, tasting periodically until they reach your desired tanginess. Perfect with sausages or as a tangy side during your camping adventures!

Nutritional Info: Calories: 20 | Fat: 0g | Carbs: 4g | Protein: 1g

WITNESS PROTECTION PICKLED EGGS

Prep: 10 mins | Cook: 10 mins | Serves: 1 jar

Cooking Function: Boil

Ingredients:

UK: 6 large eggs, 500ml vinegar, 100ml water, 50g sugar, 1 tablespoon salt, 1 teaspoon mustard seeds, 1 teaspoon black peppercorns

US: 6 large eggs, 2 cups vinegar, 1/3 cup water, 1/4 cup sugar, 1.8oz salt, 1 teaspoon mustard seeds, 1 teaspoon black peppercorns

Instructions:

1. Boil the eggs for 10 minutes, then cool them in cold water and peel.
2. In a saucepan, combine vinegar, water, sugar, salt, mustard seeds, and black peppercorns. Heat until the sugar dissolves, then remove from heat.
3. Place the peeled eggs in a sterilized jar and pour the vinegar mixture over them, ensuring they're submerged.
4. Seal and refrigerate for at least 1 week before eating. These zesty pickled eggs make a great high-protein snack during your travels!

Nutritional Info: Calories: 70 | Fat: 5g | Carbs: 3g | Protein: 6g

DEATH ROW DILL PICKLES

Prep: 15 mins | Cook: 0 mins | Serves: 4 jars
Cooking Function: No Cook
Ingredients:

UK: 1kg cucumbers (whole), 500ml distilled vinegar, 100g sugar, 50g salt, 4 cloves garlic (peeled), 2 tablespoons dill seeds, 1 tablespoon mustard seeds

US: 2.2lbs cucumbers (whole), 2 cups distilled vinegar, 1/2 cup sugar, 1.8oz salt, 4 cloves garlic (peeled), 2 tablespoons dill seeds, 1 tablespoon mustard seeds

Instructions:

1. In a bowl, combine vinegar, sugar, and salt, stirring until dissolved.
2. Pack the cucumbers into sterilized jars with garlic, dill seeds, and mustard seeds.
3. Pour the vinegar mixture over the cucumbers until fully submerged.
4. Seal and let them sit in the fridge for at least 1 week before consuming. Enjoy these crunchy pickles as a side or snack while on the road!

Nutritional Info: Calories: 50 | Fat: 0g | Carbs: 12g | Protein: 1g

HOMICIDE DETECTIVE'S HOT SAUCE

Prep: 10 mins | Cook: 15 mins | Serves: 1 jar
Cooking Function: Boil
Ingredients:

UK: 500g mixed chillies (stems removed), 250ml vinegar, 100g sugar, 1 teaspoon salt, 1 tablespoon garlic (minced)

US: 1.1lbs mixed chillies (stems removed), 1 cup vinegar, 1/2 cup sugar, 1 teaspoon salt, 1 tablespoon garlic (minced)

Instructions:

1. In a saucepan, combine chillies, vinegar, sugar, salt, and garlic. Bring to a boil, then reduce heat and simmer for 10 minutes.
2. Allow to cool slightly, then blend until smooth.
3. Transfer to a sterilized jar and seal. This hot sauce is perfect for spicing up your meals while camping or at home!

Nutritional Info: Calories: 20 | Fat: 0g | Carbs: 5g | Protein: 1g

FORENSIC FILES FERMENTED HOT SAUCE

Prep: 15 mins | Cook: 0 mins | Serves: 1 jar

Cooking Function: No Cook

Ingredients:

UK: 500g mixed chillies (stems removed), 250ml water, 20g sea salt, 1 tablespoon garlic (minced), 1 tablespoon sugar

US: 1.1lbs mixed chillies (stems removed), 1 cup water, 0.7oz sea salt, 1 tablespoon garlic (minced), 1 tablespoon sugar

Instructions:

1. In a blender, combine chillies, water, salt, garlic, and sugar, then blend until smooth.
2. Pour the mixture into a sterilized jar, leaving some space at the top for fermentation.
3. Cover with a cloth and secure with a rubber band. Let it ferment at room temperature for 5-7 days.
4. After fermentation, blend again and transfer to a sealed jar. This tangy hot sauce is excellent for adding a kick to any dish during your adventures!

Nutritional Info: Calories: 15 | Fat: 0g | Carbs: 3g | Protein: 0g

BALLISTICS REPORT BREAD AND BUTTER PICKLES

Prep: 15 mins | Cook: 10 mins | Serves: 4 jars

Cooking Function: Boil

Ingredients:

UK: 1kg cucumbers (sliced), 250ml white vinegar, 200g brown sugar, 50g salt, 1 teaspoon mustard seeds, 1 teaspoon black peppercorns

US: 2.2lbs cucumbers (sliced), 1 cup white vinegar, 1 cup brown sugar, 3.5oz salt, 1 teaspoon mustard seeds, 1 teaspoon black peppercorns

Instructions:

1. In a large bowl, mix the cucumber slices with salt and let sit for 1 hour.
2. In a saucepan, combine vinegar, sugar, mustard seeds, and black peppercorns. Heat until the sugar dissolves.
3. Rinse cucumbers and pack them into sterilized jars.
4. Pour the vinegar mixture over the cucumbers, ensuring they are submerged.
5. Seal the jars and let them cool to room temperature before refrigerating. Enjoy these sweet and tangy pickles as a side or snack during your travels!

Nutritional Info: Calories: 60 | Fat: 0g | Carbs: 15g | Protein: 1g

CORONER'S PICKLED CARROTS

Prep: 10 mins | Cook: 15 mins | Serves: 4 jars
Cooking Function: Boil
Ingredients:

UK: 500g carrots (peeled and cut into sticks), 250ml vinegar, 100g sugar, 1 tablespoon salt, 1 teaspoon mustard seeds, 1 teaspoon dill seeds

US: 1.1lbs carrots (peeled and cut into sticks), 1 cup vinegar, 1/2 cup sugar, 1.8oz salt, 1 teaspoon mustard seeds, 1 teaspoon dill seeds

Instructions:

1. In a saucepan, combine vinegar, sugar, and salt. Heat until dissolved.
2. Pack the carrot sticks into sterilized jars with mustard and dill seeds.
3. Pour the vinegar mixture over the carrots, ensuring they're submerged.
4. Seal the jars and let them cool before refrigerating. These crunchy pickled carrots are a fantastic snack or side for your campervan meals!

Nutritional Info: Calories: 45 | Fat: 0g | Carbs: 10g | Protein: 1g

EYEWITNESS PICKLED ONIONS

Prep: 10 mins | Cook: 10 mins | Serves: 1 jar
Cooking Function: Boil
Ingredients:

UK: 250g small onions (peeled), 200ml white vinegar, 100g sugar, 1 tablespoon salt, 1 teaspoon black peppercorns

US: 0.55lbs small onions (peeled), 3/4 cup white vinegar, 1/2 cup sugar, 1 tablespoon salt, 1 teaspoon black peppercorns

Instructions:

1. In a saucepan, combine vinegar, sugar, salt, and peppercorns. Heat until dissolved.
2. Place the peeled onions into a sterilized jar and pour the vinegar mixture over them.
3. Seal and let them cool before refrigerating. These tangy pickled onions are perfect as a topping for sandwiches or salads during your camping trips!

Nutritional Info: Calories: 30 | Fat: 0g | Carbs: 7g | Protein: 1g

LAST WORDS LEMON CURD

Prep: 15 mins | Cook: 15 mins | Serves: 1 jar
Cooking Function: Boil
Ingredients:

UK: 3 large eggs, 100g sugar, 100ml lemon juice, 50g butter, 1 tablespoon lemon zest

US: 3 large eggs, 1/2 cup sugar, 1/3 cup lemon juice, 3.5oz butter, 1 tablespoon lemon zest

Instructions:

1. In a saucepan, whisk together eggs, sugar, and lemon juice over low heat until well combined.
2. Stir continuously until the mixture thickens (about 5-7 minutes).
3. Remove from heat and stir in butter and lemon zest until melted and smooth.
4. Pour the lemon curd into a sterilized jar, seal, and let cool. This zesty spread is delicious on toast or as a filling for cakes while you're on the road!

Nutritional Info: Calories: 120 | Fat: 5g | Carbs: 18g | Protein: 2g

CHAPTER 9: ALIBI-WORTHY APPETIZERS

CRIME SCENE CROSTINI

Prep: 10 mins | Cook: 5 mins | Serves: 4

Cooking Function: Toast

Ingredients:

UK: 1 baguette (sliced), 100g cream cheese, 50g smoked salmon, 1 tablespoon capers, 1 tablespoon fresh dill (chopped), lemon wedges (for serving)

US: 1 baguette (sliced), 3.5oz cream cheese, 1.8oz smoked salmon, 1 tablespoon capers, 1 tablespoon fresh dill (chopped), lemon wedges (for serving)

Instructions:

1. Preheat your griddle to medium-high heat.
2. Arrange the baguette slices on the griddle and toast for about 3-5 minutes, until golden brown.
3. While the bread is toasting, mix the cream cheese with chopped dill in a bowl.
4. Once the crostini are toasted, spread a generous layer of cream cheese on each slice.
5. Top each with smoked salmon and a few capers.
6. Serve with lemon wedges on the side for a zesty finish. Enjoy your delicious Crime Scene Crostini during your next campervan adventure!

Nutritional Info: Calories: 220 | Fat: 10g | Carbs: 25g | Protein: 8g

LINEUP LETTUCE WRAPS

Prep: 15 mins | Cook: 5 mins | Serves: 4

Cooking Function: Stir-Fry

Ingredients:

UK: 500g cooked chicken (shredded), 1 tablespoon soy sauce, 1 tablespoon sesame oil, 1 tablespoon hoisin sauce, 1 head iceberg lettuce (leaves separated), 1 carrot (grated), chopped spring onions (for garnish)

US: 1.1lbs cooked chicken (shredded), 1 tablespoon soy sauce, 1 tablespoon sesame oil, 1 tablespoon hoisin sauce, 1 head iceberg lettuce (leaves separated), 1 carrot (grated), chopped spring onions (for garnish)

Instructions:

1. Heat the sesame oil in a frying pan over medium heat.

2. Add the shredded chicken and stir-fry for 3-5 minutes until heated through.

3. Stir in the soy sauce and hoisin sauce, mixing well.

4. Spoon the chicken mixture into lettuce leaves and top with grated carrot and chopped spring onions.

5. Roll them up and enjoy your Lineup Lettuce Wraps as a light and tasty appetizer!

Nutritional Info: Calories: 180 | Fat: 8g | Carbs: 5g | Protein: 25g

EYEWITNESS DEVILED EGGS

Prep: 15 mins | Cook: 10 mins | Serves: 6

Cooking Function: Boil

Ingredients:

UK: 6 large eggs, 50g mayonnaise, 1 teaspoon Dijon mustard, 1 teaspoon white vinegar, salt, pepper, paprika (for garnish)

US: 6 large eggs, 3.5oz mayonnaise, 1 teaspoon Dijon mustard, 1 teaspoon white vinegar, salt, pepper, paprika (for garnish)

Instructions:

1. Place the eggs in a saucepan and cover them with cold water. Bring to a boil over high heat.

2. Once boiling, cover and remove from heat. Let the eggs sit for 10 minutes.

3. After 10 minutes, transfer the eggs to an ice bath to cool.

4. Peel the eggs and slice them in half lengthwise. Remove the yolks and place them in a bowl.

5. Mash the yolks with mayonnaise, mustard, vinegar, salt, and pepper until smooth.

6. Spoon or pipe the mixture back into the egg whites and sprinkle with paprika. Enjoy your Eyewitness Deviled Eggs as a classic campervan snack!

Nutritional Info: Calories: 150 | Fat: 11g | Carbs: 1g | Protein: 12g

COLD CASE CAPRESE SKEWERS

Prep: 10 mins | Cook: 0 mins | Serves: 4

Cooking Function: No Cook

Ingredients:

UK: 200g cherry tomatoes, 200g mozzarella balls, 1 tablespoon fresh basil (chopped), 30ml balsamic glaze, salt, pepper

US: 7oz cherry tomatoes, 7oz mozzarella balls, 1 tablespoon fresh basil (chopped), 2 tablespoons balsamic glaze, salt, pepper

Instructions:

1. On skewers, alternate threading cherry tomatoes and mozzarella balls.
2. Once assembled, sprinkle with chopped basil, salt, and pepper.
3. Drizzle balsamic glaze over the skewers before serving. These Cold-Case Caprese Skewers are fresh and perfect for your campervan picnics!

Nutritional Info: Calories: 120 | Fat: 7g | Carbs: 8g | Protein: 6g

SHALLOW GRAVE STUFFED MUSHROOMS

Prep: 10 mins | Cook: 15 mins | Serves: 4

Cooking Function: Roast

Ingredients:

UK: 250g button mushrooms (stems removed), 100g cream cheese, 50g grated cheddar cheese, 1 garlic clove (minced), 1 tablespoon fresh parsley (chopped)

US: 0.55lbs button mushrooms (stems removed), 3.5oz cream cheese, 1.8oz grated cheddar cheese, 1 garlic clove (minced), 1 tablespoon fresh parsley (chopped)

Instructions:

1. Preheat your air fryer to 180°C (350°F).
2. In a bowl, mix the cream cheese, cheddar cheese, minced garlic, and parsley until well combined.
3. Stuff each mushroom cap with the cheese mixture and place them in the air fryer basket.
4. Cook for 12-15 minutes or until golden brown.
5. Let them cool slightly before serving. Enjoy these Shallow Grave Stuffed Mushrooms as a delightful appetizer on the road!

Nutritional Info: Calories: 170 | Fat: 13g | Carbs: 5g | Protein: 7g

RIGOR MORTIS ROLLUPS

Prep: 10 mins | Cook: 0 mins | Serves: 4

Cooking Function: No Cook

Ingredients:

UK: 4 large tortillas, 100g cream cheese, 100g sliced deli meat (ham or turkey), 1 red bell pepper (sliced), 1 tablespoon fresh spinach (chopped)

US: 4 large tortillas, 3.5oz cream cheese, 3.5oz sliced deli meat (ham or turkey), 1 red bell pepper (sliced), 1 tablespoon fresh spinach (chopped)

Instructions:

1. Spread cream cheese evenly over each tortilla.
2. Layer the deli meat, red bell pepper, and spinach on top of the cream cheese.
3. Roll each tortilla tightly and slice into bite-sized pieces.
4. Serve the Rigor Mortis Rollups as a fun and easy appetizer for your travels!

Nutritional Info: Calories: 220 | Fat: 10g | Carbs: 25g | Protein: 10g

CORPUS DELICTI QUESADILLAS

Prep: 10 mins | Cook: 10 mins | Serves: 4

Cooking Function: Fry

Ingredients:

UK: 4 large tortillas, 200g grated cheese (cheddar or mozzarella), 100g cooked chicken (shredded), 1 tablespoon taco seasoning, salsa (for serving)

US: 4 large tortillas, 7oz grated cheese (cheddar or mozzarella), 3.5oz cooked chicken (shredded), 1 tablespoon taco seasoning, salsa (for serving)

Instructions:

1. Heat a frying pan over medium heat.
2. Sprinkle half of the cheese on one half of each tortilla, followed by chicken and taco seasoning.
3. Fold the tortillas over and cook for 3-4 minutes on each side until golden and the cheese has melted.
4. Slice into wedges and serve with salsa. These Corpus Delicti Quesadillas are a tasty and satisfying treat on the road!

Nutritional Info: Calories: 310 | Fat: 15g | Carbs: 28g | Protein: 18g

DEADLY NIGHTSHADE NACHOS

Prep: 10 mins | Cook: 10 mins | Serves: 4

Cooking Function: Bake

Ingredients:

UK: 200g tortilla chips, 150g grated cheese (cheddar or Monterey Jack), 100g black beans (drained), 1 jalapeño (sliced), sour cream (for serving)

US: 7oz tortilla chips, 5.3oz grated cheese (cheddar or Monterey Jack), 3.5oz black beans (drained), 1 jalapeño (sliced), sour cream (for serving)

Instructions:

1. Preheat your air fryer to 200°C (400°F).
2. Spread the tortilla chips in an even layer in the air fryer basket.
3. Top with cheese, black beans, and jalapeños.
4. Bake for 5-10 minutes until the cheese is bubbly.
5. Serve warm with sour cream. These Deadly Nightshade Nachos are a must-have for your camping snack!

Nutritional Info: Calories: 300 | Fat: 18g | Carbs: 32g | Protein: 10g

STAKEOUT STUFFED PEPPERS

Prep: 15 mins | Cook: 20 mins | Serves: 4

Cooking Function: Roast

Ingredients:

UK: 4 bell peppers (halved and seeded), 200g cooked rice, 100g minced meat (beef or turkey), 1 teaspoon Italian seasoning, 50g grated cheese (for topping)

US: 4 bell peppers (halved and seeded), 7oz cooked rice, 3.5oz minced meat (beef or turkey), 1 teaspoon Italian seasoning, 1.8oz grated cheese (for topping)

Instructions:

1. Preheat your air fryer to 180°C (350°F).
2. In a bowl, mix cooked rice, minced meat, and Italian seasoning until well combined.
3. Stuff the mixture into the halved bell peppers and place them in the air fryer basket.
4. Sprinkle cheese on top and cook for 15-20 minutes until the peppers are tender.
5. Enjoy your Stakeout Stuffed Peppers as a hearty appetizer!

Nutritional Info: Calories: 250 | Fat: 12g | Carbs: 25g | Protein: 15g

UNDERCOVER AGENT AVOCADO TOAST

Prep: 5 mins | Cook: 0 mins | Serves: 2

Cooking Function: No Cook

Ingredients:

UK: 2 slices of bread (toasted), 1 ripe avocado, 1 tablespoon lemon juice, salt, pepper, chilli flakes (for garnish)

US: 2 slices of bread (toasted), 1 ripe avocado, 1 tablespoon lemon juice, salt, pepper, chilli flakes (for garnish)

Instructions:

1. In a bowl, mash the avocado with lemon juice, salt, and pepper.
2. Spread the mixture evenly on the toasted bread slices.
3. Sprinkle with chilli flakes for a spicy kick. Enjoy your Undercover Agent Avocado Toast as a fresh and quick snack while camping!

Nutritional Info: Calories: 230 | Fat: 15g | Carbs: 20g | Protein: 4g

BREAKING BRUSCHETTA

Prep: 10 mins | Cook: 5 mins | Serves: 4

Cooking Function: Toast

Ingredients:

UK: 1 baguette (sliced), 2 large tomatoes (diced), 2 garlic cloves (minced), 1 tablespoon fresh basil (chopped), 30ml olive oil, salt, pepper

US: 1 baguette (sliced), 2 large tomatoes (diced), 2 garlic cloves (minced), 1 tablespoon fresh basil (chopped), 2 tablespoons olive oil, salt, pepper

Instructions:

1. Preheat your griddle to medium heat.
2. Toast the baguette slices for 3-5 minutes until golden.
3. In a bowl, mix diced tomatoes, garlic, basil, olive oil, salt, and pepper.
4. Top each toasted slice with the tomato mixture. Enjoy your Breaking Bruschetta as a perfect campervan appetizer!

Nutritional Info: Calories: 150 | Fat: 7g | Carbs: 19g | Protein: 4g

MISDEMEANOR MEATBALLS

Prep: 15 mins | Cook: 20 mins | Serves: 4

Cooking Function: Bake

Ingredients:

UK: 500g minced meat (beef or turkey), 50g breadcrumbs, 1 egg, 2 garlic cloves (minced), 1 teaspoon Italian seasoning, salt, pepper

US: 1.1lbs minced meat (beef or turkey), 1.8oz breadcrumbs, 1 egg, 2 garlic cloves (minced), 1 teaspoon Italian seasoning, salt, pepper

Instructions:

1. Preheat your air fryer to 180°C (350°F).
2. In a bowl, mix minced meat, breadcrumbs, egg, garlic, Italian seasoning, salt, and pepper until well combined.
3. Shape the mixture into meatballs and place them in the air fryer basket.
4. Cook for 15-20 minutes until browned and cooked through. Serve your Misdemeanor Meatballs as a tasty appetizer for any gathering!

Nutritional Info: Calories: 290 | Fat: 18g | Carbs: 10g | Protein: 24g

PROBABLE CAUSE POTATO SKINS

Prep: 15 mins | Cook: 15 mins | Serves: 4

Cooking Function: Bake

Ingredients:

UK: 4 medium potatoes (baked and halved), 100g grated cheese (cheddar), 100g cooked bacon (chopped), sour cream (for serving), chopped chives (for garnish)

US: 4 medium potatoes (baked and halved), 3.5oz grated cheese (cheddar), 3.5oz cooked bacon (chopped), sour cream (for serving), chopped chives (for garnish)

Instructions:

1. Preheat your air fryer to 200°C (400°F).

2. Scoop out a bit of the potato flesh from each half, leaving a thin layer.

3. Fill each skin with cheese and bacon.

4. Air fry for 10-15 minutes until the cheese is melted and bubbly.

5. Serve with sour cream and garnish with chives. Enjoy your Probable Cause Potato Skins as a fantastic campervan snack!

Nutritional Info: Calories: 350 | Fat: 22g | Carbs: 30g | Protein: 14g

DEATH IN VENICE RISOTTO

Prep: 10 mins | Cook: 30 mins | Serves: 4
Cooking Function: Cook
Ingredients:

UK: 300g Arborio rice, 1 onion (finely chopped), 2 garlic cloves (minced), 100ml white wine, 1L vegetable stock, 100g Parmesan cheese (grated), 50g butter, salt, pepper, chopped fresh parsley (for garnish)

US: 10.5oz Arborio rice, 1 onion (finely chopped), 2 garlic cloves (minced), 3.4oz white wine, 4.2 cups vegetable stock, 3.5oz Parmesan cheese (grated), 3.5oz butter, salt, pepper, chopped fresh parsley (for garnish)

Instructions:

1. In a saucepan, melt the butter over medium heat. Add the onion and garlic, cooking until soft.
2. Stir in the Arborio rice, coating it with the butter for about 2 minutes until slightly translucent.
3. Pour in the white wine and let it simmer until mostly absorbed.
4. Gradually add the vegetable stock, one ladle at a time, stirring continuously until absorbed before adding more. This should take about 20 minutes.
5. Once the rice is creamy and al dente, stir in the Parmesan cheese. Season with salt and pepper to taste.
6. Serve the Death in Venice Risotto hot, garnished with fresh parsley. Enjoy a taste of Italy in your campervan!

Nutritional Info: Calories: 450 | Fat: 20g | Carbs: 55g | Protein: 12g

TOKYO DRIFT TERIYAKI STIR-FRY

Prep: 15 mins | Cook: 10 mins | Serves: 2
Cooking Function: Stir-Fry
Ingredients:

UK: 250g chicken breast (sliced), 150g broccoli florets, 100g bell pepper (sliced), 50g snap peas, 50ml teriyaki sauce, 1 tablespoon sesame oil, 2 spring onions (sliced), sesame seeds (for garnish)

US: 8.8oz chicken breast (sliced), 5.3oz broccoli florets, 3.5oz bell pepper (sliced), 3.5oz snap peas, 1.7oz teriyaki sauce, 1 tablespoon sesame oil, 2 spring onions (sliced), sesame seeds (for garnish)

Instructions:

1. Heat the sesame oil in a large pan over medium-high heat.
2. Add the chicken slices and cook for about 5 minutes until browned.
3. Toss in the broccoli, bell pepper, and snap peas, stirring for another 3-4 minutes until the vegetables are tender-crisp.
4. Pour the teriyaki sauce over the chicken and vegetables, stirring to coat everything evenly.
5. Cook for an additional minute until the sauce thickens slightly.
6. Serve the Tokyo Drift Teriyaki Stir-Fry hot, garnished with sliced spring onions and sesame seeds. A quick and delicious meal for your campervan adventure!

Nutritional Info: Calories: 300 | Fat: 10g | Carbs: 25g | Protein: 30g

MOROCCAN MURDER MYSTERY TAGINE

Prep: 20 mins | Cook: 1 hour | Serves: 4

Cooking Function: Stew

Ingredients:

UK: 500g lamb (cubed), 1 onion (chopped), 2 garlic cloves (minced), 1 teaspoon ground cumin, 1 teaspoon ground cinnamon, 400g chopped tomatoes (canned), 200g chickpeas (drained), 100g dried apricots (chopped), 500ml chicken stock, salt, pepper, fresh coriander (for garnish)

US: 1.1lbs lamb (cubed), 1 onion (chopped), 2 garlic cloves (minced), 1 teaspoon ground cumin, 1 teaspoon ground cinnamon, 14oz chopped tomatoes (canned), 7oz chickpeas (drained), 3.5oz dried apricots (chopped), 2 cups chicken stock, salt, pepper, fresh coriander (for garnish)

Instructions:

1. In a large pot, brown the lamb cubes over medium heat until browned on all sides.
2. Add the chopped onion and garlic, cooking until softened.
3. Stir in the cumin and cinnamon, cooking for another minute until fragrant.
4. Add the chopped tomatoes, chickpeas, dried apricots, and chicken stock. Bring to a boil.
5. Reduce the heat and let it simmer for about 45 minutes until the lamb is tender.
6. Serve the Moroccan Murder Mystery Tagine hot, garnished with fresh coriander. A hearty meal perfect for chilling out in your campervan!

Nutritional Info: Calories: 550 | Fat: 30g | Carbs: 40g | Protein: 35g

GREEK TRAGEDY GYROS

Prep: 15 mins | Cook: 15 mins | Serves: 4
Cooking Function: Roast
Ingredients:

UK: 500g chicken thighs (sliced), 1 teaspoon dried oregano, 1 teaspoon garlic powder, 4 pita bread, 200g tzatziki sauce, 100g cherry tomatoes (halved), 100g cucumber (sliced), salt, pepper

US: 1.1lbs chicken thighs (sliced), 1 teaspoon dried oregano, 1 teaspoon garlic powder, 4 pita bread, 7oz tzatziki sauce, 3.5oz cherry tomatoes (halved), 3.5oz cucumber (sliced), salt, pepper

Instructions:

1. Preheat your air fryer to 200°C (400°F).
2. In a bowl, toss the chicken with oregano, garlic powder, salt, and pepper until coated.
3. Place the chicken in the air fryer basket and roast for about 12-15 minutes until cooked through.
4. Warm the pita bread in the air fryer for the last 2 minutes.
5. Assemble the gyros by filling each pita with chicken, tzatziki, cherry tomatoes, and cucumber.
6. Serve the Greek Tragedy Gyros warm, and enjoy this tasty, portable meal on your camping trip!

Nutritional Info: Calories: 450 | Fat: 18g | Carbs: 45g | Protein: 30g

INDIAN CONSPIRACY CURRY

Prep: 10 mins | Cook: 30 mins | Serves: 4
Cooking Function: Stew
Ingredients:

UK: 400g chicken breast (diced), 1 onion (chopped), 2 garlic cloves (minced), 1 tablespoon curry powder, 400ml coconut milk, 200g spinach, salt, pepper, cooked rice (to serve)

US: 14oz chicken breast (diced), 1 onion (chopped), 2 garlic cloves (minced), 1 tablespoon curry powder, 14oz coconut milk, 7oz spinach, salt, pepper, cooked rice (to serve)

Instructions:

1. In a pot, sauté the onion and garlic until softened.
2. Add the chicken and cook until no longer pink.
3. Stir in the curry powder, coating the chicken.
4. Pour in the coconut milk and bring to a simmer.
5. Add the spinach and cook for an additional 5 minutes until wilted.
6. Serve the Indian Conspiracy Curry over cooked rice for a warming meal in your campervan!

Nutritional Info: Calories: 400 | Fat: 22g | Carbs: 25g | Protein: 25g

MEXICAN STANDOFF ENCHILADAS

Prep: 20 mins | Cook: 25 mins | Serves: 4

Cooking Function: Bake

Ingredients:

UK: 8 corn tortillas, 300g cooked chicken (shredded), 400g enchilada sauce, 100g cheese (grated), 100g black beans (drained), 1 avocado (sliced), fresh coriander (for garnish)

US: 8 corn tortillas, 10.5oz cooked chicken (shredded), 14oz enchilada sauce, 3.5oz cheese (grated), 3.5oz black beans (drained), 1 avocado (sliced), fresh coriander (for garnish)

Instructions:

1. Preheat your air fryer to 180°C (350°F).
2. Fill each tortilla with chicken and black beans, rolling them up tightly.
3. Place the enchiladas seam-side down in a baking dish.
4. Pour the enchilada sauce over the top and sprinkle with cheese.
5. Bake for about 20 minutes until the cheese is melted and bubbly.
6. Serve the Mexican Standoff Enchiladas hot, garnished with avocado and coriander for a fiesta in your campervan!

Nutritional Info: Calories: 450 | Fat: 25g | Carbs: 35g | Protein: 30g

FRENCH CONNECTION RATATOUILLE

Prep: 15 mins | Cook: 30 mins | Serves: 4
Cooking Function: Roast
Ingredients:

UK: 1 aubergine (cubed), 1 courgette (sliced), 1 bell pepper (chopped), 1 onion (chopped), 400g chopped tomatoes (canned), 2 garlic cloves (minced), 1 teaspoon dried thyme, salt, pepper, fresh basil (for garnish)

US: 1 eggplant (cubed), 1 zucchini (sliced), 1 bell pepper (chopped), 1 onion (chopped), 14oz chopped tomatoes (canned), 2 garlic cloves (minced), 1 teaspoon dried thyme, salt, pepper, fresh basil (for garnish)

Instructions:

1. Preheat your air fryer to 200°C (400°F).
2. In a large bowl, toss all the vegetables with garlic, thyme, salt, and pepper.
3. Spread the mixture in the air fryer basket in a single layer.
4. Roast for about 25-30 minutes, shaking the basket halfway through.
5. Serve the French Connection Ratatouille hot, garnished with fresh basil. This classic dish brings a taste of France to your campervan!

Nutritional Info: Calories: 250 | Fat: 5g | Carbs: 45g | Protein: 6g

ITALIAN JOB PASTA PUTTANESCA

Prep: 10 mins | Cook: 15 mins | Serves: 4
Cooking Function: Boil
Ingredients:

UK: 300g spaghetti, 1 can (400g) chopped tomatoes, 50g black olives (sliced), 2 anchovy fillets (chopped), 2 garlic cloves (minced), 1 teaspoon dried oregano, salt, pepper, fresh parsley (for garnish)

US: 10.5oz spaghetti, 14oz chopped tomatoes, 1.8oz black olives (sliced), 2 anchovy fillets (chopped), 2 garlic cloves (minced), 1 teaspoon dried oregano, salt, pepper, fresh parsley (for garnish)

Instructions:

1. Boil a pot of salted water and cook the spaghetti according to package instructions until al dente.
2. In a separate pan, heat a splash of olive oil and sauté the garlic and anchovies until fragrant.
3. Add the chopped tomatoes, olives, oregano, salt, and pepper. Let it simmer for about 5 minutes.
4. Drain the spaghetti and mix it with the sauce.
5. Serve the Italian Job Pasta Puttanesca hot, garnished with fresh parsley. A quick and flavourful dish for your campervan dinners!

Nutritional Info: Calories: 350 | Fat: 10g | Carbs: 60g | Protein: 12g

SPANISH INQUISITION PAELLA

Prep: 15 mins | Cook: 30 mins | Serves: 4
Cooking Function: Stew
Ingredients:

UK: 300g paella rice, 400g chicken thighs (diced), 200g prawns (peeled), 1 bell pepper (chopped), 100g peas (frozen), 1 onion (chopped), 2 garlic cloves (minced), 1 teaspoon smoked paprika, 1L chicken stock, salt, pepper, lemon wedges (to serve)

US: 10.5oz paella rice, 14oz chicken thighs (diced), 7oz prawns (peeled), 1 bell pepper (chopped), 3.5oz peas (frozen), 1 onion (chopped), 2 garlic cloves (minced), 1 teaspoon smoked paprika, 4.2 cups chicken stock, salt, pepper, lemon wedges (to serve)

Instructions:

1. In a large pot, sauté the onion and garlic until softened.
2. Add the chicken and cook until browned.
3. Stir in the rice and smoked paprika, coating everything well.
4. Pour in the chicken stock and bring to a simmer.
5. Add the bell pepper and peas, cooking for about 20 minutes until the rice is tender.
6. Top with prawns in the last 5 minutes. Serve the Spanish Inquisition Paella with lemon wedges for a sunny feast in your campervan!

Nutritional Info: Calories: 500 | Fat: 15g | Carbs: 65g | Protein: 25g

GERMAN NOIR SCHNITZEL

Prep: 10 mins | Cook: 15 mins | Serves: 4

Cooking Function: Fry

Ingredients:

UK: 500g pork loin (sliced thin), 100g breadcrumbs, 50g flour, 2 eggs (beaten), salt, pepper, vegetable oil (for frying), lemon wedges (to serve)

US: 1.1lbs pork loin (sliced thin), 3.5oz breadcrumbs, 1.8oz flour, 2 eggs (beaten), salt, pepper, vegetable oil (for frying), lemon wedges (to serve)

Instructions:

1. Season the flour with salt and pepper. Dredge each pork slice in flour, then dip in the beaten eggs, and finally coat with breadcrumbs.

2. In a frying pan, heat vegetable oil over medium-high heat.

3. Fry the schnitzels for about 3-4 minutes on each side until golden and cooked through.

4. Drain on paper towels and serve the German Noir Schnitzel hot with lemon wedges. This classic dish will be a hit on your camping trip!

Nutritional Info: Calories: 600 | Fat: 35g | Carbs: 45g | Protein: 40g

THAI CRIME WAVE GREEN CURRY

Prep: 10 mins | Cook: 20 mins | Serves: 4

Cooking Function: Stew

Ingredients:

UK: 400g chicken breast (sliced), 1 can (400ml) coconut milk, 2 tablespoons green curry paste, 200g green beans (trimmed), 100g baby corn (sliced), 1 tablespoon fish sauce, fresh basil (for garnish)

US: 14oz chicken breast (sliced), 14oz coconut milk, 2 tablespoons green curry paste, 7oz green beans (trimmed), 3.5oz baby corn (sliced), 1 tablespoon fish sauce, fresh basil (for garnish)

Instructions:

1. In a pot, heat the green curry paste over medium heat until fragrant.

2. Add the coconut milk and stir well to combine.

3. Toss in the chicken slices, cooking until no longer pink.

4. Add the green beans and baby corn, simmering for about 10 minutes until tender.

5. Stir in the fish sauce and serve the Thai Crime Wave Green Curry hot, garnished with fresh basil. Perfect for a spicy adventure in your campervan!

Nutritional Info: Calories: 450 | Fat: 30g | Carbs: 10g | Protein: 35g

AMERICAN PSYCHO BURGER

Prep: 10 mins | Cook: 15 mins | Serves: 4
Cooking Function: Grill
Ingredients:

UK: 500g minced beef, 1 teaspoon smoked paprika, 1 teaspoon garlic powder, salt, pepper, 4 burger buns, 4 slices cheese, lettuce, tomato, onion (for serving)

US: 1.1lbs minced beef, 1 teaspoon smoked paprika, 1 teaspoon garlic powder, salt, pepper, 4 burger buns, 4 slices cheese, lettuce, tomato, onion (for serving)

Instructions:

1. In a bowl, combine the minced beef with smoked paprika, garlic powder, salt, and pepper.
2. Form the mixture into 4 patties.
3. Preheat your grill and cook the patties for about 6-7 minutes on each side until cooked to your liking.
4. Add a slice of cheese on top during the last minute of cooking to melt.
5. Serve the American Psycho Burger on a bun with lettuce, tomato, and onion. A deliciously juicy treat for your campervan meals!

Nutritional Info: Calories: 600 | Fat: 35g | Carbs: 40g | Protein: 45g

BRITISH BAKE-OFF OR DIE SCONES

Prep: 15 mins | Cook: 20 mins | Serves: 8
Cooking Function: Bake
Ingredients:

UK: 225g self-raising flour, 50g butter (cubed), 25g sugar, 150ml milk, 1 egg (beaten, for glazing)

US: 8oz self-raising flour, 1.8oz butter (cubed), 0.9oz sugar, 5.1oz milk, 1 egg (beaten, for glazing)

Instructions:

1. Preheat your oven to 220°C (425°F).
2. In a bowl, rub the butter into the flour until it resembles breadcrumbs.
3. Stir in the sugar and make a well in the centre.
4. Gradually add the milk, mixing until a dough forms.
5. Turn the dough onto a floured surface and roll out to about 2cm thick. Cut out scones using a cutter.
6. Place on a baking tray, glaze with beaten egg, and bake for 15-20 minutes until golden. Serve the British Bake-Off or Die Scones warm with jam and cream!

Nutritional Info: Calories: 200 | Fat: 8g | Carbs: 30g | Protein: 5g

MEASUREMENT CONVERSIONS

When you're cooking in a campervan, you might not always have your full set of measuring tools on hand. Here's a quick conversion guide to help you out in a pinch. Remember, these are approximate conversions for precise baking, it's always best to weigh ingredients when possible.

VOLUME CONVERSIONS

Metric	Imperial
5 ml	1 teaspoon
15 ml	1 tablespoon
60 ml	1/4 cup
80 ml	1/3 cup
125 ml	1/2 cup
250 ml	1 cup
500 ml	2 cups / 1 pint
1 litre	4 cups / 2 pints

WEIGHT CONVERSIONS

Metric	Imperial
28 g	1 oz
100 g	3.5 oz
225 g	8 oz / 1/2 lb
450 g	16 oz / 1 lb
1 kg	2.2 lb

OVEN TEMPERATURE CONVERSIONS

Celsius (Fan)	Celsius (Conventional)	Gas Mark	Fahrenheit
140°C	160°C	3	325°F
150°C	170°C	4	350°F
170°C	190°C	5	375°F
180°C	200°C	6	400°F
190°C	210°C	7	425°F
200°C	220°C	8	450°F

REMEMBER:

Always use a food thermometer to check temperatures.

Insert the thermometer into the thickest part of the meat, away from bone, fat, or gristle.

For whole poultry, check the temperature in the innermost part of the thigh and wing, and the thickest part of the breast.

Let meat rest for 3 minutes before carving or consuming.

MEAL PLANNING TEMPLATES

Meal planning is key to successful campervan cooking. Here's a 60-day meal plan for your Campervans, Cooking, and Corpses theme, organized by weeks, with each day categorized into breakfast, lunch, appetizer, dinner, and a special Sunday dinner to help you plan your culinary adventures.

WEEK 1

DAYS	BREAKFAST	LUNCH	Appetizer	DINNER
MONDAY	Alibi Avocado Toast	Cold Case Pasta Salad	Crime Scene Crostini	One-Pot Prison Break Pasta
TUESDAY	Corpse-Cold Overnight Oats	Stashed Cash Sandwich	Eyewitness Deviled Eggs	Lethal Injection Lemon Chicken
WEDNESDAY	Smuggler's Breakfast Burrito	Poison Ivy Pesto Wrap	Lineup Lettuce Wraps	Rigor Mortis Risotto
THURSDAY	Detective's Delight Pancakes	Evidence Bag Quinoa Bowl	Cold Case Caprese Skewers	Last Meal Lasagna
FRIDAY	Stakeout Shakshuka	Misdemeanor Minestrone	Shallow Grave Stuffed Mushrooms	Shallow Grave Shepherd's Pie
SATURDAY	Witness Protection Waffles	Conspiracy Theory Couscous Salad	Corpus Delicti Quesadillas	Arsenic and Old Lace Casserole
SUNDAY (SPECIAL DINNER)	Fingerprint Fruit Salad	Getaway Car Gazpacho	Undercover Agent Avocado Toast	Cyanide Surprise Cheesecake (No-Bake)

WEEK 2

DAYS	BREAKFAST	LUNCH	Appetizer	DINNER
MONDAY	Undercover Granola	Witness Statement White Bean Dip	Deadly Nightshade Nachos	Mob Boss Meatballs
TUESDAY	Body Bag Breakfast Porridge	Ransom Note Ramen	Breaking Bruschetta	Penal Code Pesto Salmon
WEDNESDAY	Coroner's Coffee Cake	Undercover Agent Egg Salad	Misdemeanor Meatballs	Homicide Detective's Hotpot
THURSDAY	Chalk Outline Chia Pudding	Buried Treasure Baked Potato	Cold Trail Cucumber Salad	Forensic Files Fajitas
FRIDAY	Alibi Avocado Toast	Smoke Screen Stuffed Peppers	Planted Evidence Popcorn	Death Row Ratatouille
SATURDAY	Corpse-Cold Overnight Oats	Lineup Lentil Soup	Stakeout Stuffed Peppers	Hanging Judge Halloumi Skewers
SUNDAY (SPECIAL DINNER)	Smuggler's Breakfast Burrito	Cold Case Pasta Salad	Eyewitness Account Edamame	Last Gasp Lemon Bars

WEEK 3

DAYS	BREAKFAST	LUNCH	Appetizer	DINNER
MONDAY	Detective's Delight Pancakes	Evidence Bag Quinoa Bowl	Wiretap Wontons	Death in Venice Risotto
TUESDAY	Stakeout Shakshuka	Poison Ivy Pesto Wrap	Lineup Potato Wedges	Tokyo Drift Teriyaki Stir-Fry
WEDNESDAY	Witness Protection Waffles	Conspiracy Theory Couscous Salad	Confidential Informant Cheese Dip	Moroccan Murder Mystery Tagine
THURSDAY	Fingerprint Fruit Salad	Getaway Car Gazpacho	Planted Evidence Pea Salad	Greek Tragedy Gyros
FRIDAY	Undercover Granola	Ransom Note Ramen	Breaking Breadsticks	Indian Conspiracy Curry
SATURDAY	Body Bag Breakfast Porridge	Buried Treasure Baked Potato	Undercover Hummus	Mexican Standoff Enchiladas
SUNDAY (SPECIAL DINNER)	Coroner's Coffee Cake	Lineup Lentil Soup	Crime Scene Crostini	Shallow Grave S'mores

WEEK 4

DAYS	BREAKFAST	LUNCH	Appetizer	DINNER
MONDAY	Alibi Avocado Toast	Stashed Cash Sandwich	Eyewitness Deviled Eggs	Last Meal Lasagna
TUESDAY	Corpse-Cold Overnight Oats	Poison Ivy Pesto Wrap	Lineup Lettuce Wraps	Rigor Mortis Risotto
WEDNESDAY	Smuggler's Breakfast Burrito	Evidence Bag Quinoa Bowl	Cold Case Caprese Skewers	Lethal Injection Lemon Chicken
THURSDAY	Detective's Delight Pancakes	Misdemeanor Minestrone	Shallow Grave Stuffed Mushrooms	Shallow Grave Shepherd's Pie
FRIDAY	Stakeout Shakshuka	Witness Statement White Bean Dip	Corpus Delicti Quesadillas	Cement Shoes Seafood Stew
SATURDAY	Witness Protection Waffles	Conspiracy Theory Couscous Salad	Deadly Nightshade Nachos	Mob Boss Meatballs
SUNDAY (SPECIAL DINNER)	Fingerprint Fruit Salad	Getaway Car Gazpacho	Undercover Agent Avocado Toast	Death by Chocolate Mousse

WEEK 5

DAYS	BREAKFAST	LUNCH	Appetizer	DINNER
MONDAY	Undercover Granola	Witness Statement White Bean Dip	Crime Scene Crostini	One-Pot Prison Break Pasta
TUESDAY	Body Bag Breakfast Porridge	Ransom Note Ramen	Eyewitness Account Edamame	Lethal Injection Lava Cake
WEDNESDAY	Coroner's Coffee Cake	Undercover Agent Egg Salad	Misdemeanor Meatballs	Homicide Detective's Hotpot
THURSDAY	Chalk Outline Chia Pudding	Buried Treasure Baked Potato	Cold Trail Cucumber Salad	Forensic Files Fajitas
FRIDAY	Alibi Avocado Toast	Smoke Screen Stuffed Peppers	Planted Evidence Popcorn	Death Row Ratatouille
SATURDAY	Corpse-Cold Overnight Oats	Lineup Lentil Soup	Stakeout Stuffed Peppers	Hanging Judge Halloumi Skewers
SUNDAY (SPECIAL DINNER)	Smuggler's Breakfast Burrito	Cold Case Pasta Salad	Eyewitness Account Edamame	Last Gasp Lemon Bars

WEEK 6

DAYS	BREAKFAST	LUNCH	Appetizer	DINNER
MONDAY	Detective's Delight Pancakes	Evidence Bag Quinoa Bowl	Wiretap Wontons	Death in Venice Risotto
TUESDAY	Stakeout Shakshuka	Poison Ivy Pesto Wrap	Lineup Potato Wedges	Tokyo Drift Teriyaki Stir-Fry
WEDNESDAY	Witness Protection Waffles	Conspiracy Theory Couscous Salad	Confidential Informant Cheese Dip	Moroccan Murder Mystery Tagine
THURSDAY	Fingerprint Fruit Salad	Getaway Car Gazpacho	Planted Evidence Pea Salad	Greek Tragedy Gyros
FRIDAY	Undercover Granola	Ransom Note Ramen	Breaking Breadsticks	Indian Conspiracy Curry
SATURDAY	Body Bag Breakfast Porridge	Buried Treasure Baked Potato	Undercover Hummus	Mexican Standoff Enchiladas
SUNDAY (SPECIAL DINNER)	Coroner's Coffee Cake	Lineup Lentil Soup	Crime Scene Crostini	Shallow Grave S'mores

WEEK 7

DAYS	BREAKFAST	LUNCH	Appetizer	DINNER
MONDAY	Alibi Apple Cinnamon Oatmeal	Double Life Veggie Wrap	Coroner's Corn Fritters	Suspect Stir-Fried Tofu with Vegetables
TUESDAY	Mysterious Melon Medley	Evidence-Driven Egg Salad	Undercover Buffalo Cauliflower	Silent Witness Seared Salmon
WEDNESDAY	Conspiracy Croissant Sandwich	Ransom Note Quinoa Salad	Cold Case Cucumber Rolls	Unsolved Mystery Mushroom Risotto
THURSDAY	Crime Scene Smoothie Bowl	Undercover Taco Salad	Stashed Cash Spinach Dip	Witness Protection Chicken Stir-Fry
FRIDAY	Dead Man's Toast with Avocado	No More Lies Lentil Wrap	Alibi Asparagus Fries	Fatal Attraction Fettuccine Alfredo
SATURDAY	Body Language Banana Pancakes	Scent of a Crime Shrimp Tacos	Alibi Artichoke Dip	Homicidal Honey Garlic Chicken
SUNDAY (SPECIAL DINNER)	Chalk Outline Chia Bowl	Getaway Gazpacho	Corpse-cold antipasto Platter	Macabre Mint Chocolate Chip Ice Cream

WEEK 8

DAYS	BREAKFAST	LUNCH	Appetizer	DINNER
MONDAY	Alibi Almond Butter Toast	Cold Case Couscous Salad	Lineup Loaded Nachos	Stolen Treasure Stuffed Peppers
TUESDAY	Witness Protection Smoothie	Ransom Note Rice Bowl	Sly Spy Spinach Salad	Pulp Fiction BBQ Ribs
WEDNESDAY	Conspiracy Theory Yogurt Parfait	Cold Case Chicken Caesar Wrap	Undercover Vegetable Tempura	Suspicious Stew
THURSDAY	Detective's Daily Fruit Bowl	Witness Statement Wrap	Homicidal Hummus	Crime Scene Chili
FRIDAY	Mortuary Muffins	Fatal Flavors Taco Bowl	Criminally Good Cheese Platter	Last Resort Grilled Shrimp
SATURDAY	Blood Orange Smoothie	Double-Cross Veggie Sandwich	Accused Avocado Hummus	Under Investigation Vegetable Curry
SUNDAY (SPECIAL DINNER)	Crypt Keeper's Breakfast Burrito	Getaway Salad	No Alibi Nachos	Whodunit Whipped Cheesecake

WEEK 9

DAYS	BREAKFAST	LUNCH	Appetizer	DINNER
MONDAY	Undercover Granola	Witness Statement White Bean Dip	Deadly Nightshade Nachos	Mob Boss Meatballs
TUESDAY	Body Bag Breakfast Porridge	Ransom Note Ramen	Breaking Bruschetta	Penal Code Pesto Salmon
WEDNESDAY	Coroner's Coffee Cake	Undercover Agent Egg Salad	Misdemeanor Meatballs	Homicide Detective's Hotpot
THURSDAY	Chalk Outline Chia Pudding	Buried Treasure Baked Potato	Cold Trail Cucumber Salad	Forensic Files Fajitas

This completes your 60-day meal plan! Each week includes a variety of breakfast, lunch, appetiser, dinner, and special occasion options, all themed around Campervans, Cooking, and Corpses. Remember to include recipes for your favourite meal or adjust as you enjoy the meal plan.

TIPS FOR USING THESE TEMPLATES:

1. switch your favourite meal ideas first.
2. List all ingredients needed for each meal.
3. Cross-reference with what you already have in your campervan.
4. Create your shopping list from the remaining items.
5. Remember to include staples like oil, salt, and spices in your planning.

HAPPY PLANNING, AND MAY ALL YOUR MEALS BE DELICIOUSLY MYSTERIOUS!

Made in United States
Troutdale, OR
12/22/2024

27109759R00066